Land's End to John O'Groats
End to End Cycle Route
A Safer Way

First published 2014
·This edition 2021

© 2014 Royston Wood

The Moral right of the author has been asserted.

Dedication

This book is dedicated to all those that have lost their lives whilst cycling from one end of the country to the other and the loved ones they have left behind.

Figure 1 - Devon Red Rubies (in Worcestershire)

Contents

Figure 2 - St Mary's Church, Kidderminster

Warning

This book is not a traditional guide book: it is not intended as a standalone step by step written guide.

The book is an accompaniment to the main product which is a series of eighteen gpx files designed to guide you across the country using a satellite navigation device or a smart phone or similar device that can navigate using gpx files. (See Chapter One for instruction on how to download the GPX files.)

The whole route from Land's End to John O'Groats has been broken into eighteen sections of approximately 50 miles each. It is intended that the files are loaded into a satellite navigation device (sat nav), smart phone or other device capable of reading the files. The files would then be used consecutively to journey from one end of the country to the other.

The eighteen route segments are also available as maps in Google Maps (see Appendix One). This will enable you to view the route on a zoomable map to see the course in detail. You can also view in satellite mode to get some idea of terrain.

Chapter Two also gives instructions on how to amend the gpx files to suit your own needs.

The book contains a brief description of each section of the route with maps to aid navigation. Please note that these maps are not particularly detailed due to their scale. Unfortunately if maps of sufficient detail to be fully navigable were included the book would be as thick as a block of gold and similarly expensive.

However, I refer you again to the links to the route on Google Maps (see Appendix One). If you have a portable device with Google Maps functionality you can access the maps en-route if necessary.

The book also contains a list of accommodation

available along the route. There are many places to stay along or within a short cycle of the route. I have listed accommodation at roughly 20-25 mile steps. To keep the book to a manageable size I have selected two Bed & Breakfast (B&B) establishments and one camping site (where available) at each point.

There is also a chapter listing bike shops close to the route. A couple of them are mobile services and they may be able to rescue you in an emergency if you are fairly close by. Please note that I haven't actually asked them if they will do this but it would be worth a shot!

A final warning - this route has off road sections. They are not real 'off road', mainly canal paths with various surfaces ranging from tarmac through cinder to bare earth and grass. I have ridden the route on a road bike to show that it is a feasible route. However, if you only want to ride on tarmac then this is not the route for you.

By the time I pushed my weight down on the pedals and glided away from the John O'Groats signpost at the start of my first end to end, back in 2009, I had spent a lot of time planning, plotting and training. A lot more time than I would spend of the ride itself.

In all that planning I had spent precious little time thinking about safety. In fact I had devised a route that utilised busy main roads, many of which were dual carriageways. The route was designed for speed because I only had six days in which to complete the ride.

It wasn't that I was ignoring safety. To ignore something you have to be conscious that it is there in the first place. The thing is, it didn't enter my head that my proposed route could be dangerous. I was living in the invulnerability bubble that many cyclists inhabit before it is burst by an errant driver, wandering dog or meandering sheep.

Since 2009 I have been knocked from my bike twice. The first time was by a car driver making a right hand turn right in front of me, without indicating. I could tell he wasn't looking either because he was more shocked than me when I came smashing through his passenger window. The second incident was more serious and potentially lethal. Commuting home I was smashed from my bike by a lorry after the driver decided to change lanes from the outside lane, through the inside lane and into the cycle lane!

Then came the news of two fatalities on the A30: end to end charity cyclists on their first day. I had cycled along the A30 through half of Devon and all of Cornwall in the erroneous belief that if I kept behind the solid white line at the edge of the road it would keep me safe from the traffic. The lorry driver that mowed the end to enders down was asleep and took little notice of the white line. Its protective force field did not bounce the lorry back either.

If you are not aware of it already I have a website all about planning and preparing for the end to end ride (**www.landsend-to-johnogroats.co.uk**). The route on the site, although not suggested for riding, is the route I rode in 2009. I have become increasingly concerned that someone might try to follow that route and end up under a lorry.

So, my last two end to end rides have been a quest to find a safer route for cyclists.

Okay, it wasn't hard to find a safer route than my original one but I wanted one as safe as possible, without detouring miles and miles away from a relatively straight line.

The difficulty was knowing where to start (yes, yes, I know: Land's End or John O'Groats, ha ha). It was impossible to know which of the squiggles on the map were the safest. I started by eliminating the obviously dangerous ones and then trying to find minor roads that shadowed them. The trouble was that perhaps those roads acted as feeder roads and would be just as busy, especially near junctions.

I spent some time on the forums looking for safe suggestions but started to lose hours. The problem was I only had a short time to come up with a route because, in my usual impetuous style, I had decided to test ride the route the next week. If I left it any longer the winter would have been upon me and I would have to wait until spring.

When I went to Google Maps to start some serious plotting I discovered that they had just started beta testing cycle routing. I typed in Land's End to John

O'Groats and asked for the route. Ping! Two seconds later a suggested route appeared.

I decided to use it. My reasoning was that it could take hours and hours of research and work to devise a route of my own. I could use those hours and hours to ride the suggested route as an exercise in primary research.

That is what happened. I rode the route. The story of my experiences on the ride is contained in my book: Land's End to John O'Groats – Cycling the Google Route. The route was 90 % excellent and 10% lethal. It utilised very minor roads, old railway lines, canal paths and the odd footpath. Unfortunately it seemed to link these together using major A roads and dual carriageways!

Whilst much better than my 2009 route it was not ready for publication. So, I took the excellent 90% and re-routed the dodgy 10%. On paper the route looked good so I re-rode it in the late spring, crossing the country for the second time in a few months.

The resultant route was brilliant, although you should be aware of the caveats (sorry, I am an ex lawyer) below.

The route has a number of off road sections, mainly canal paths. Whilst most of the canal paths were in really good condition with surfaces much better than some of the minor lanes, others were not. Some sections were not tarmacked or gritted and I imagine they could become quite muddy. The canal paths were, however, some of the quietest riding I have ever done.

I have not commented on the specific surfaces of each particular canal path because they will change over time. When I rode through some cinder tracks were in the process of being tarmacked but at the same time some tarmacked sections were in the process of being taken back by nature. As a general rule, the paths become less well surfaced the further north you travel.

The bike I rode was a pure road bike: a Cube Agree

GTC Pro. The only concession I made to the route was to use some fairly puncture proof tyres. I would recommend Schwalbe Marathons or Vittoria Randonneurs. The latter are lighter weight, a less rigid ride and normally cheaper but the Schwalbe's possibly have the edge on puncture resistance.

If you are unlucky enough to come across a section that is impassable you should be able to navigate around the obstruction. I have set out instructions on how to do this using a Garmin 800 in Appendix Two. Other devices will probably have similar functions.

Whilst you are safe from sleeping lorry drivers on the canal paths you should be aware of other potential dangers, such as riding into the canal and drowning, mad swans and errant ducks (the last two possible resulting in the first).

Figure 3 - Danger of Death, A9 Drumochter Pass
(Route Uses a Cycle Path)

Chapter One

Downloading the GPX Files

The gpx files can be downloaded from here:
http://www.landsend-to-johnogroats.co.uk/gpx-files

Click on the ZIP button and a zipped folder containing the eighteen gpx files will be downloaded to your computer or device. How this occurs will depend upon the settings of your particular computer or device. In most instances the zip folder will be found in your 'downloads' folder. If your device does not automatically extract the individual files from the zipped folder you will need to do this manually. The method will depend on your device. For instance, on most PCs double clicking on the file should activate the zip extraction tool. If not, right click and look for an extract or open option. If in doubt you may need to consult the help facility on your device.

When you try to open the files your device will probably inform you that it has no program to view them. This is because gpx file are made to be viewed on a navigation device. You need to load them onto the device that you intend to navigate with. I have not given instruction on how to do this because each device will be different so you will need to refer to the instructions for the device.

If you would like to see the route on a map I would suggest that you use the links in Appendix One to view the route sections in Google Maps. This will allow you to zoom in and out to see the route in detail. You can also view the route in satellite mode to get some idea of terrain.

If you would like to amend the gpx files on a map I would recommend using www.bikehike.co.uk. Instructions on how to do this are contained in Chapter Two.

You can also download a pdf version of the book, which might be useful. The maps will be in colour and you can zoom in to see details a little better (although using the Google Map links in Appendix One would be better).

Click on the PDF button and the file should automatically download to your computer or device. You will need an app such as Adobe Reader in order to be able to read the file. This comes as a standard on most computers but there is a download link on the page should you require it. For handheld devices you may need to download a suitable app from your app store.

If all else fails you can contact the author on royston.wood@live.co.uk

Figure 4 - Dunrobin Castle Railway Station, Golspie

Chapter Two

Amending the GPX Files

If you would like to amend the gpx route I would recommend using www.bikehike.co.uk. If you are unfamiliar with the website use the following instructions:

1. Click on the hyperlink above (or type the URL into your browser for non-interactive formats).

2. Click on Course Creator (see Picture One). This will open the map screen. There should be a large map and a small map with Mapping Control below it.

Picture One

3. In the Mapping Control click on Load Route (see Picture Two)

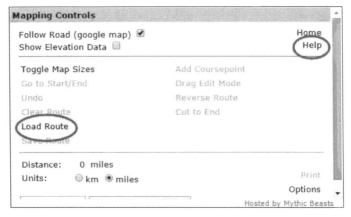

Picture Two

4. In the pop up box click Choose File. Browse for the file you would like to open, select it and click Open. Now click on Upload Route (see Picture Three).

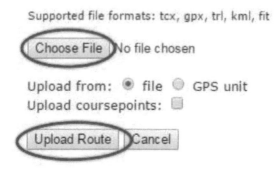

Picture Three

There are comprehensive instructions on amending the route at www.bikehike.co.uk/help.php. Amongst other features you will be able to:

- Amend the course by dragging the line.
- Reverse the route
- Merge routes
- Add points of interest
- View and add elevation data

You can save the route at any point by clicking Save Route in the Mapping Controls below Load Route.

You can then select the file type you would like to save as (if unsure choose gpx route), give the file a meaningful name and then click Download Route. The route will download to your download folder. Open the folder and cut or copy the file to your desired location. Alternatively select to you can download direct to your gps device.

Chapter Three

The Route

This route is designed to keep the rider on as quiet a route as possible whilst still keeping to a fairly straight line between Land's End and John O'Groats.

Whilst the route uses paths that are not 'road' it does not stray to anything that would be determined as strictly 'off road'. The author has ridden the route on a road bike, the only concession made to the route was shoeing the bike with tough tyres (Schwalbe Marathons on first trip and Vittoria Randonneurs on second).

The route is intended for use as gpx files with a navigation device. The maps that follow are intended purely to give a visual representation. In most cases they do not have sufficient detail to enable navigation by the maps alone. Links to scalable maps in Google Maps can be found in Appendix One.

The route is broken into eighteen sections of approximately 50 miles each. It is not intended that you break your journey at the end of each section, it is merely broken at regular intervals for convenience. Load the relevant file for your current position on the ride and when you reach the end of the section load the next file. If you stop for the night part way through a route section simple reload it when you start the next day and your device should pick up your location and where you are on the route.

You may wish to amend the route to match your planned days' routes. This can be done using the instruction contained in Chapter Two.

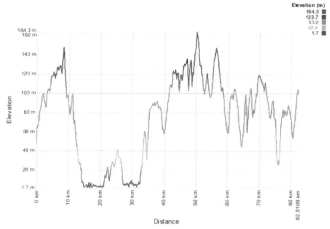

The standard joke about which direction to ride end to end is that if you start in John O'Groats it is all downhill. In fact, if you took out all the ups and downs between the two points there would be a slight slope downwards from Land's End to John O'Groats. This is because you start at the top of a cliff and finish at a little above sea level.

That's the end of the good news. The start is generally uphill for the first five miles or so before you descend towards Newlyn and the sea. The cycle path along Penzance sea front takes you towards St Michael's Mount, which makes a fine focal point, providing the sea mist isn't blocking the view. A short hop over the hills to traverse the peninsula at its narrowest point takes you from the south coast to Hayle on the north coast via very quiet lanes.

More quiet lanes and cycle paths follow to Cambourne with a similar pattern to Redruth. There are a few steep ups and downs with a general progression of up.

After Redruth the route's profile becomes more jagged with many short sharp climbs along quiet lanes. On the whole it is not too heavy going but as can be seen from the route profile, there is very little that could be considered as flat.

Figure 5 - St Michael's Mount, Marazion, nr Penzance

LEJOG 1 – Whole - Lands End to Whitecross

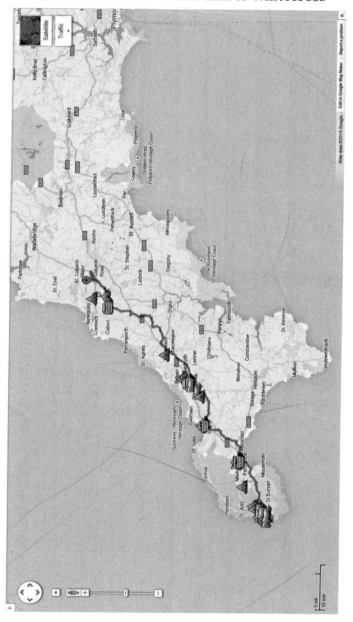

LEJOG 1 – 1

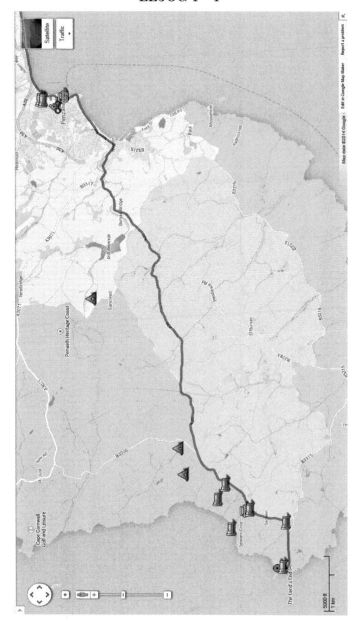

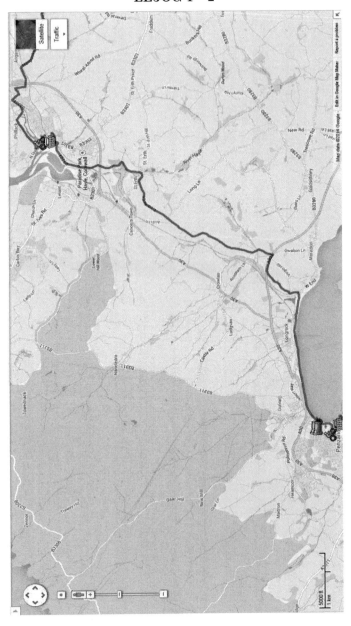

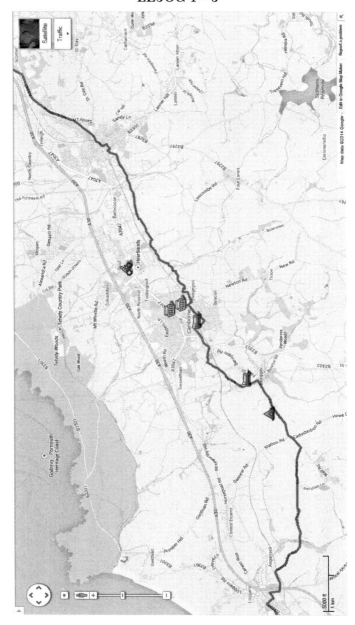

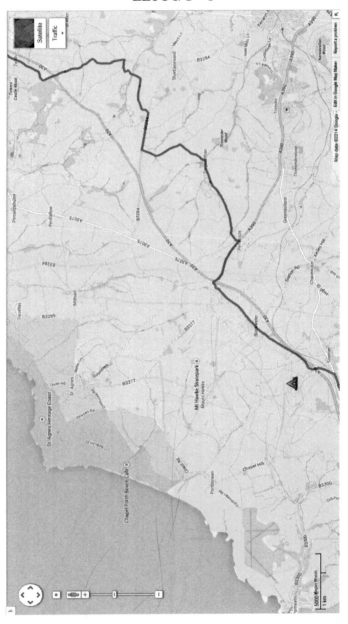

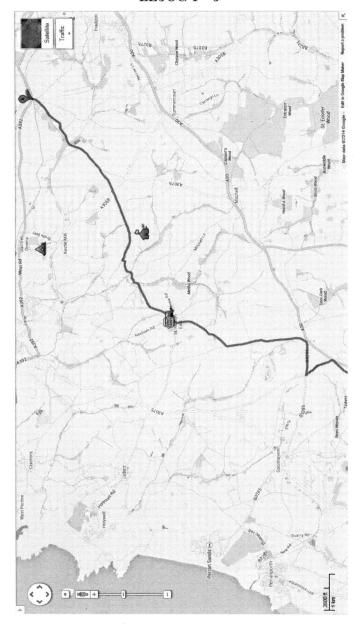

LEJOG 2
Whitecross to Hatherleigh

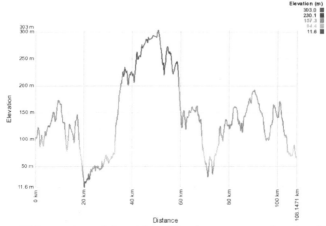

This section of the ride will take you over the shoulder of Bodmin Moor, out of Cornwall and into north Devon.

The first ten miles of the route continue to follow quiet lanes, bumping up and down some short but stiff climbs. Then the route descends steeply to join the Camel Trail (no, sorry, no Camels – it is named after the nearby River Camel).

The Camel Trail is a cycle way that is followed for eight miles, climbing almost continually at a small gradient. In total the whole 'climb' is 40m. At the end of the trail you immediately hit a 10% hill and climb the same in the next 400 metres, which is followed by quite a bit more climbing up to the edge of Bodmin Moor. You can clearly see this at about the 35 km point on the elevation profile.

The moor is exposed compared to the largely sheltered lanes so far on the route. It is also covered in dozy sheep that have a tendency to meander out in front of cyclists.

The descent from the Bodmin Moor is fast and at times technical but exhilarating. Thereafter the route follows mainly quiet lanes into Devon.

The hills of north Devon are tough with nothing approaching flat; it is either up or down and it mostly feels up. After passing through Holsworthy the route follows an off road path. The gpx may try to turn you a little too soon. If so climb up the hill a little further before turning onto the path. If you would prefer to avoid the path you can continue on the road for approximately three and a half miles, until you pick up the route again.

From that point the route follows the A3072 for a few miles over some rolling terrain before heading onto another cycle track almost into Hatherleigh and the end of the section. Again, you could stay on the main road until Hatherleigh if you would prefer.

Figure 6 - Cornish Flag

LEJOG 2 –Whitecross to Hatherleigh

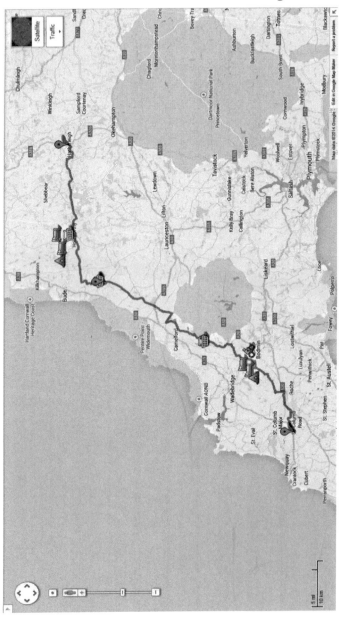

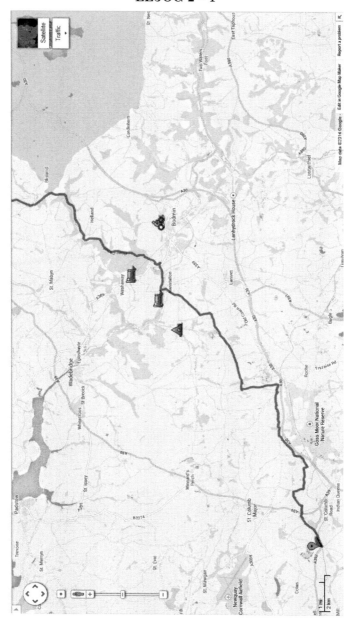

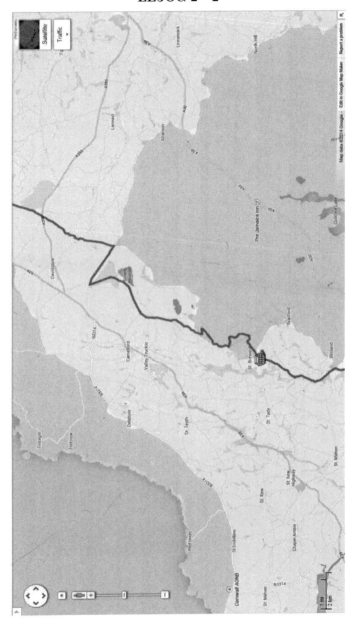

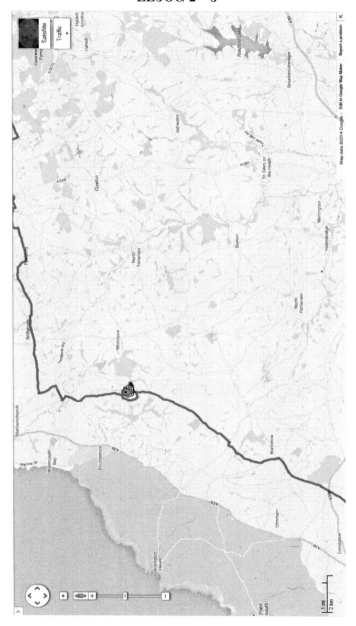

LEJOG 2 – 4

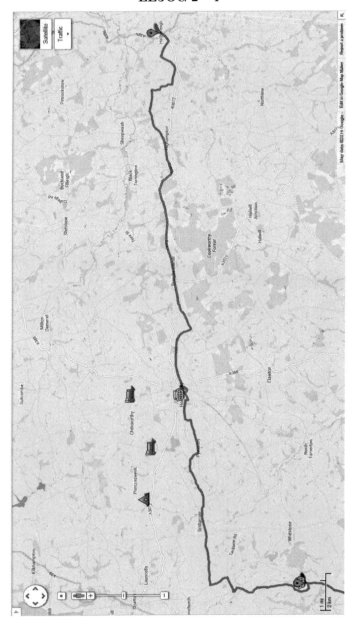

LEJOG 3
Hatherleigh to Taunton

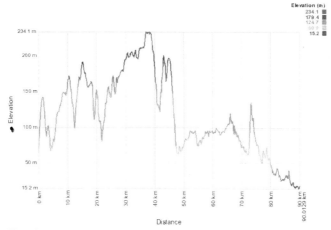

The third section of the route is a ride of two parts: the first slogging through the hills of Devon and the second cruising along the flat lanes and paths of Somerset. The profile map shows the distinction, Tiverton being at approximately the 47 km point.

The hilly bit begins instantly with a stiff climb out of Hatherleigh but the effort is rewarded with some magnificent views. If you feel like a break in Hatherleigh I would recommend waiting until the top of the climb where benches await.

The first thirty miles are some of the toughest on the whole end to end. Everytime you grapple your way to the top of a climb you plunge down the other side and then immediately start climbing again. The lanes are very quiet though and, to be frank, that's Devon for you.

If you begin to despair keep in the forefront of your mind that once you reach Tiverton it is pretty flat for the next couple of sections.

The relief comes a couple of miles before Tiverton at the top of the appropriately named Long Drag Hill. This gloriously fast, straight descent drops you all the way to the outskirts of Tiverton, where you will be directed the wrong way down the one way pedestrianised main street. This might prove to be a bit of a hinderence if it is busy but has the advantages of putting you in amongst the shops and avoiding some busy roads on the one way system.

The route between Tiverton and Taunton uses a mix of old railway lines, canal paths and quiet roads. Taunton itself is quite difficult to navigate. It has a complex one way system so the route uses a number of cycle paths. Stick to the line of the gpx and it will guide you through to the start of the canal at Firepool Lock.

Figure 7 - Firepool Lock, Taunton

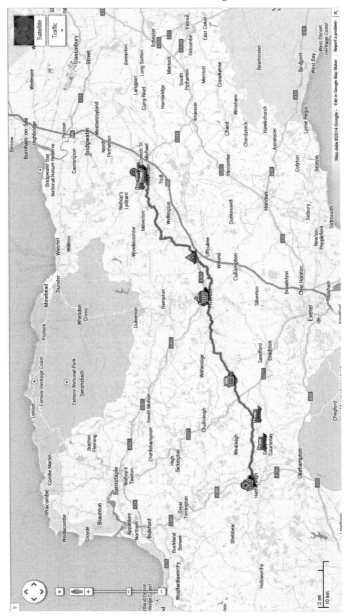

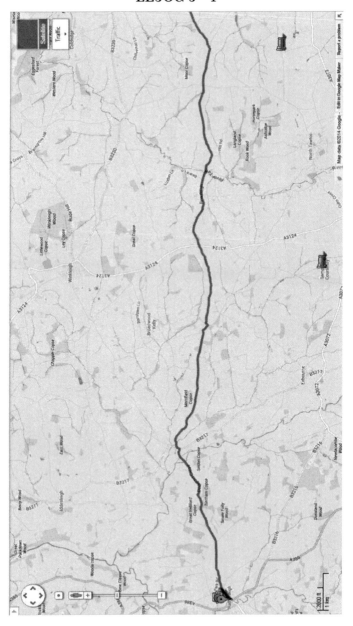

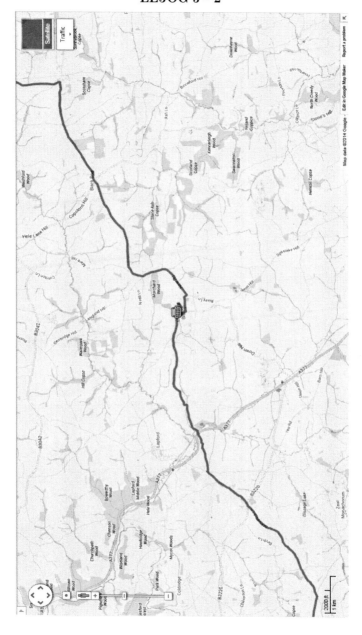

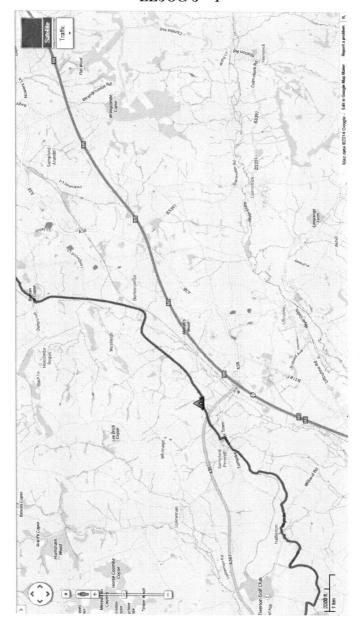

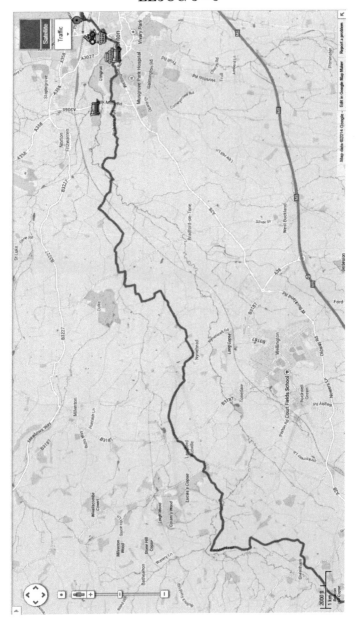

LEJOG 4
Taunton to Clevedon

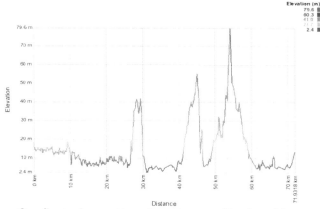

On first glance the elevation profile for this section makes it look like it has three massive peaks. However, a closer inspection of the scale will show a different story: the biggest 'peak' is a gain of about eighty metres over roughly 6 km. The reason for the distortion is because the bits between the hills are canal paths and old railway lines. Despite the jagged nature shown on the profile these are flat, as might be expected.

This is possibly the easiest section on the whole ride and is a just reward for dragging yourself all the way through Cornwall and Devon, probably the hardest part of the ride.

The first few miles are spent on the Bridgwater and Taunton Canal towpath, which appropriately enough, leads you from Taunton to Bridgwater. From Bridwater the route follows quiet lanes through the Somerset Levels to Cheddar. The land has been reclaimed from marshland and the lanes are characterised by many 90° turns as the road follows the drainage ditches.

Shortly after Cheddar the route joins an old railway line. This forms part of the Strawberry Line Cycle Way and is followed to the end of this section in Clevedon. The cycle way uses old railway lines where possible, linked by quiet lanes.

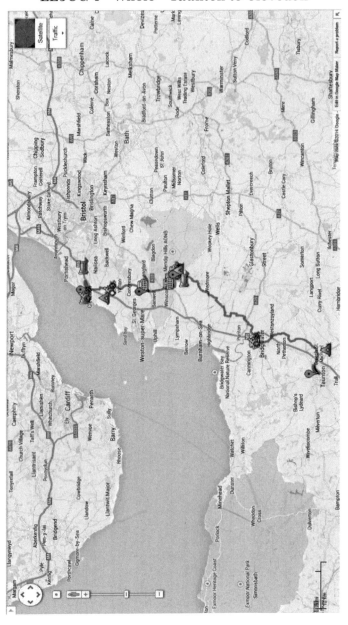

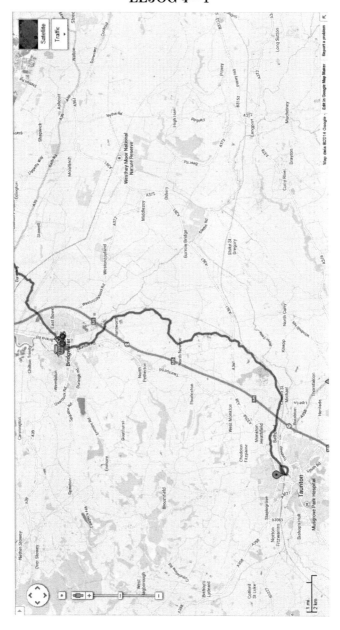

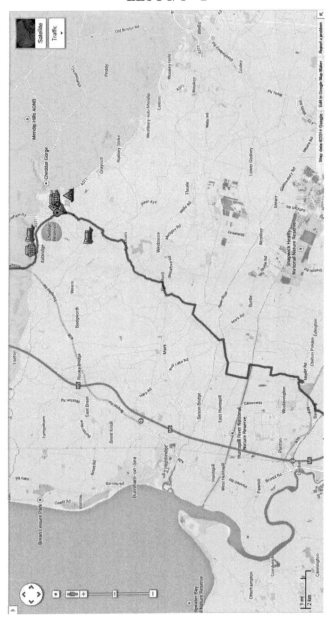

LEJOG 4 – 3

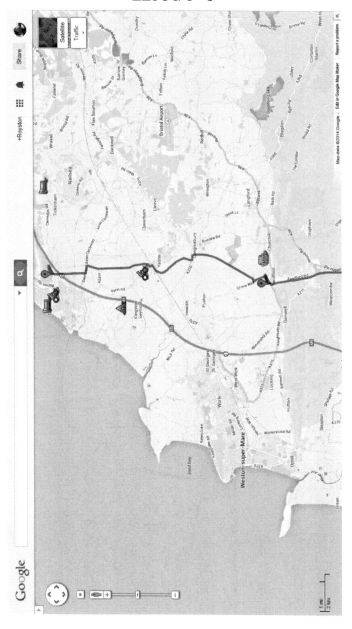

43

LEJOG 5
Clevedon to Gloucester

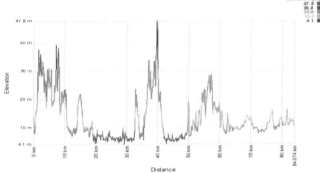

Again, the profile looks jagged but the scale reveals the truth – this is a mostly flat section, not even rising to an elevation of more than fifty metres above sea level.

Initially the route shadows the M5 but at a much lower elevation and on a virtually traffic free lane. After passing under the M5 a few times and using various lanes and paths the route joins the M5. Do not be alarmed, there is a cycleway, completely separate from the road itself, that uses the M5 bridge to cross the River Avon.

A network of lanes and paths are used to traverse the industrialised area around Avonmouth before the route joins quiet lanes for several miles leading to the Gloucester and Sharpness Canal. Apart from a small detour through the village of Frampton on Severn the canal tow path is followed all the way to the end of the section, in Gloucester.

Figure 8 – Swing Bridge, Gloucester and Sharpness Canal

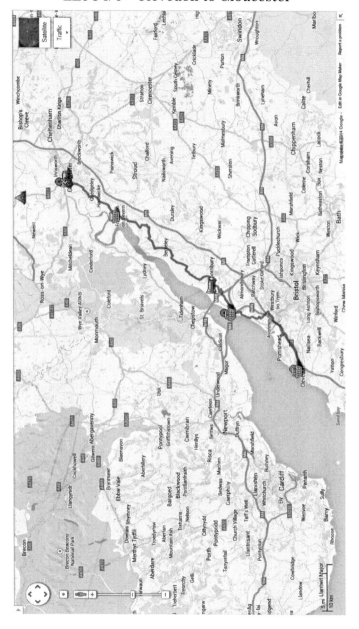

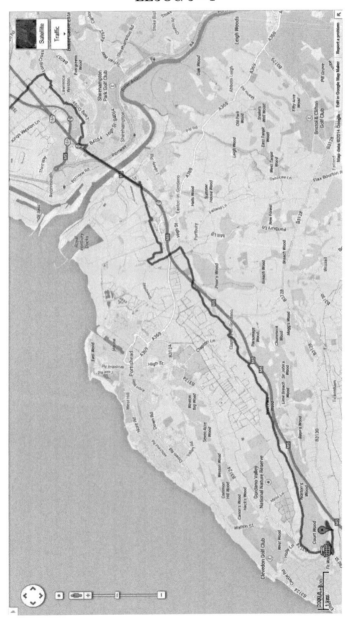

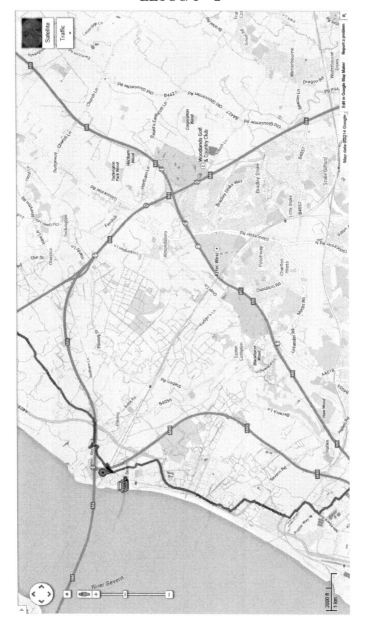

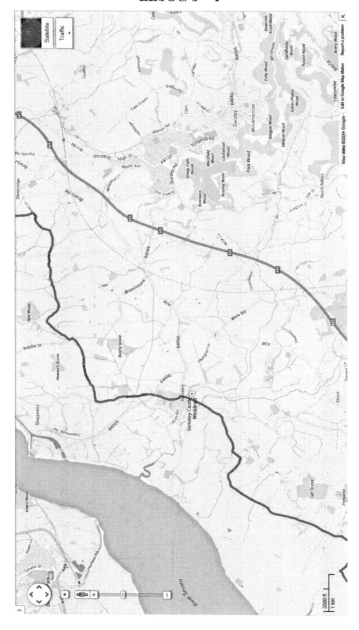

LEJOG 5 – 6

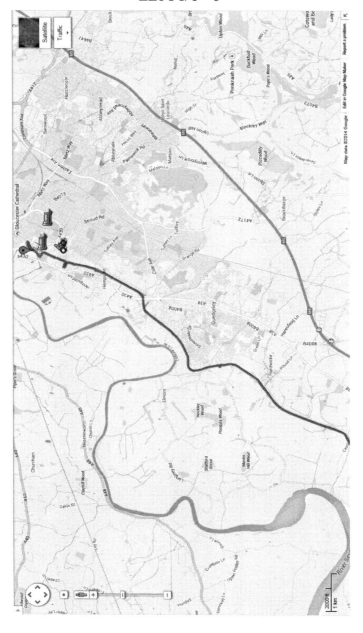

LEJOG 6
Gloucester to Kidderminster

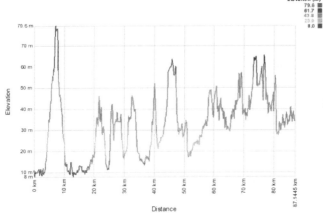

It is back to the hills for a while but don't worry, they are not as bad as those in Devon.

A cycle way and quiet lanes lead you away from Gloucester towards Tewksebury, passing some historic buildings on the way. Originally the route tried to cross the River Severn just outside Tewksebury without using a bridge. It has now been re-routed by the only route possible without a major detour, via the A438 and the A38. Whilst not madly busy the A38 is potentially the busiest road on the route so far. Thankfully within a couple of miles the route turns onto quiet but choppy lanes, which are followed into Worcester.

Worcester is traversed on the tow path of the Worcester and Birmingham Canal to re-join quiet lanes and roads through Droitwich Spa and on towards Kidderminster.

A few miles short of Kidderminster the route passes though the Harlebury Trading Estate, going through several no entry signs. The trading estate is very quiet and this should not prove an obstacle.

After the trading estate there is a short but memorably steep climb before a few twists and turns leads you onto a cycle path that utilises an old railway line. This in turn leads to the Staffordshire and Worcestershire Canal which will be followed to the end of the section in Kidderminster.

LEJOG 6 – Gloucester to Kidderminster

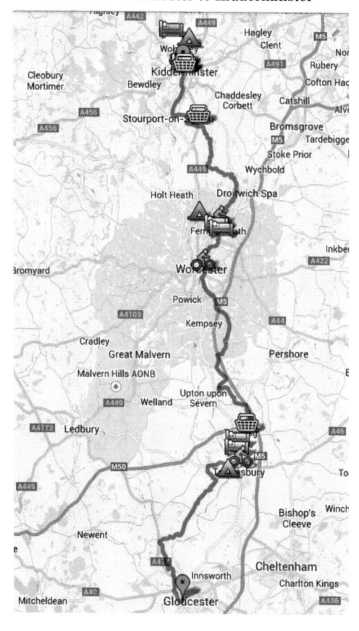

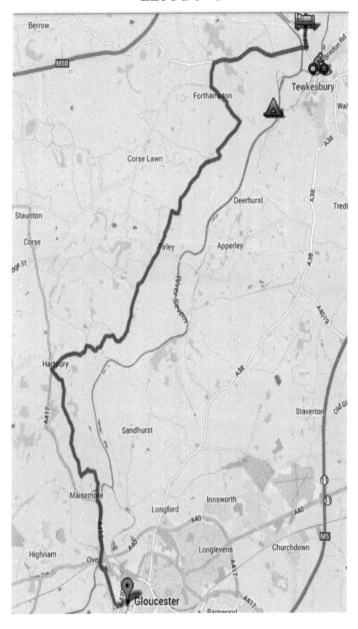

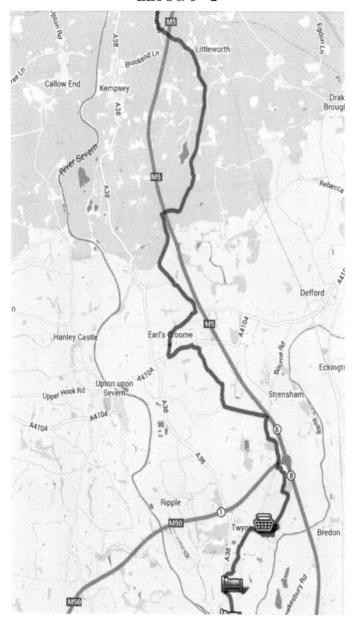

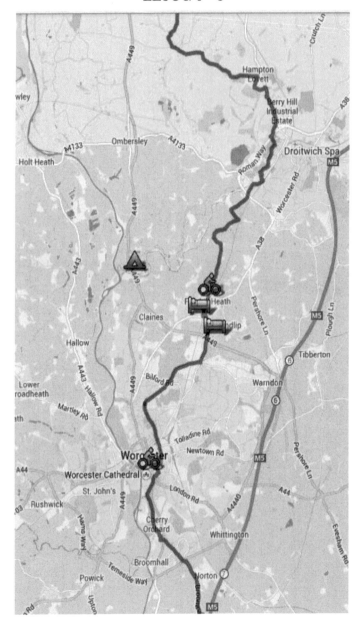

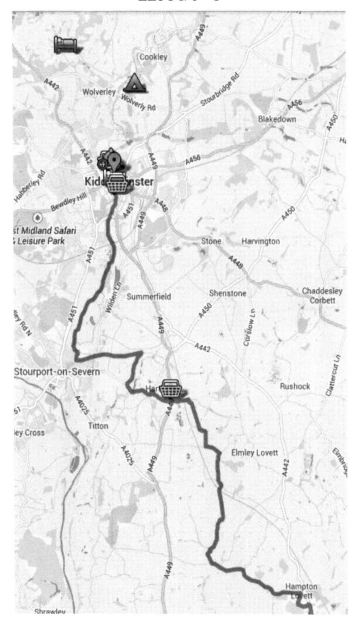

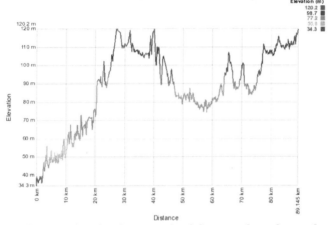

This section is characterised by canal paths and old railways. There are a couple of major roads but these have good cycle lanes. The profile is misleading, this section being predominantly flat.

From Kidderminster the route continues along the Staffordshire and Worcestershire Canal to Wombourne where it links via road to the South Staffordshire Railway Walk. This is followed for a few miles to the Shropshire Union Canal. Quiet roads then lead through Penkridge to join the Staffordshire and Worcestershire canal into Stafford.

After one busy junction Stafford is traversed on quiet back roads and paths. Leaving Stafford the route follows alongside the A513 on a cycle path for about half a mile before hopping via quite lanes to the A34. Here there is another cycle path counter flowing the traffic (but very separated from it).

The Trent and Mersey Canal is then followed to the end of the section in Stoke-on-Trent.

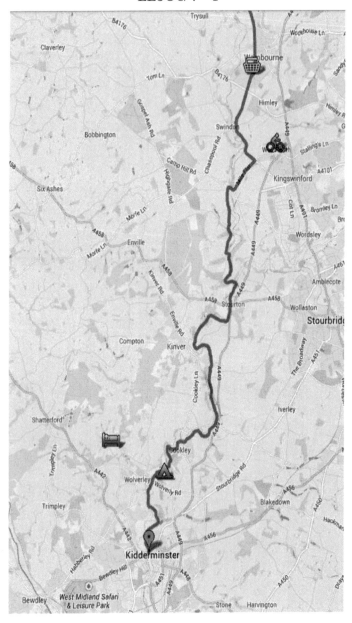

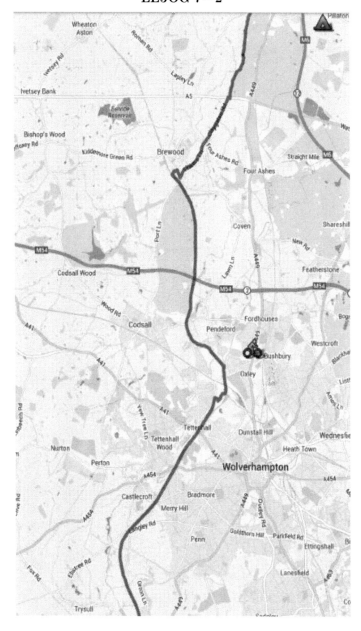

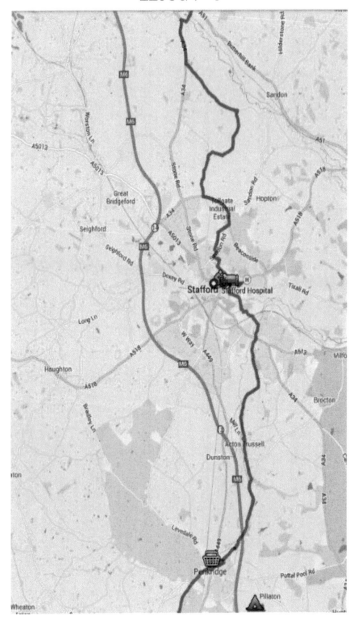

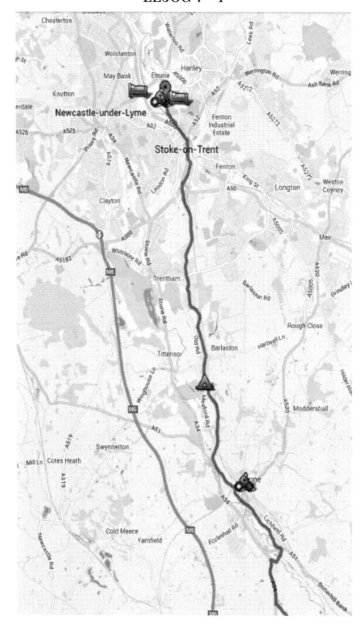

LEJOG 8
Stoke-on-Trent to Hindley

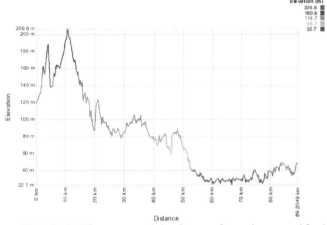

This feels like a surprisingly rural section considering the urban landscape that is being crossed. The route uses a multitude of roads, lanes, paths and canal paths and you may have to stop several times to negotiate cycle calming barriers.

Leaving the canal path soon after the start, the route follows roads to link with Whitfield Valley Greenway cycle way. The cycle way leads to Congleton from where the route follows lanes to Wilmslow.

In Wilmslow the route cuts from the road and follows a path along the river. Whilst this is a pleasant detour it does mean carrying your bike up a fair number of steps in a steep path to rejoin the road. If this does not appeal you can stick to the road. Continue up Cliff Road before turning left onto Styal Road. This will rejoin with the route in a little over half a mile.

The route continues along this road for several miles before joining small lanes to link with a cycle path through Kenworthy Woods. The path runs alongside the River Mersey, past Stretford Cemetery to join the Bridgewater Canal. The towpath leads to the junction with the Manchester Ship Canal, which is crossed by bridge.

The route then continues along roads through Eccles to re-join the Bridgewater Canal for a short distance before emerging onto mainly back roads leading to the A580. There is a separate cycle path on this dual carriageway, which is followed for a short distance before turning onto quieter roads.

After a couple of miles the route joins a cycle way which it follows to the end of the section in Hindley.

Figure 9 - Black and White House, Bridgewater Canal

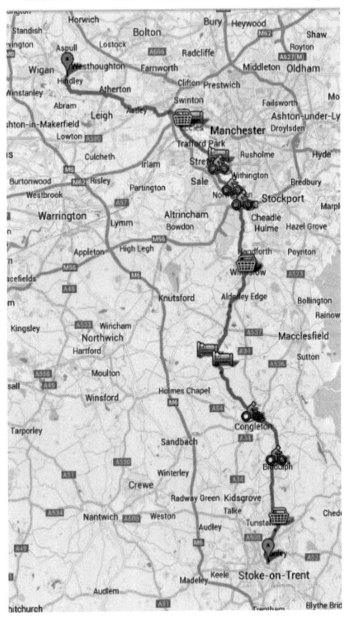

LEJOG 8 – 1

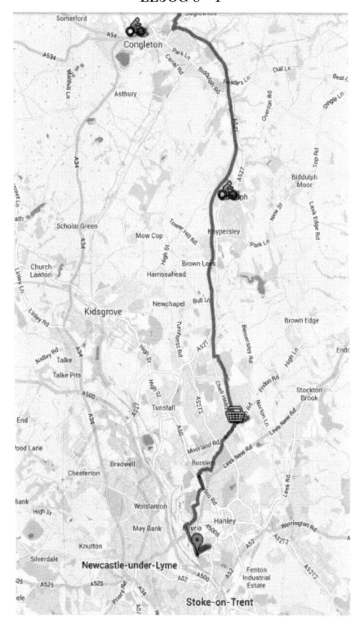

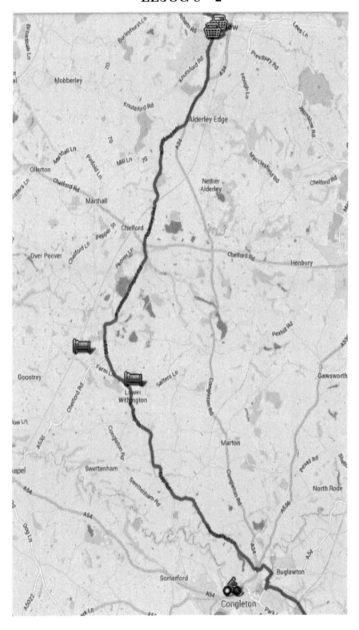

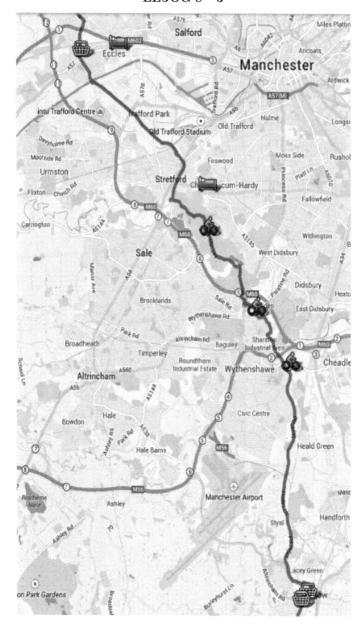

LEJOG 9
Hindley to Lancaster

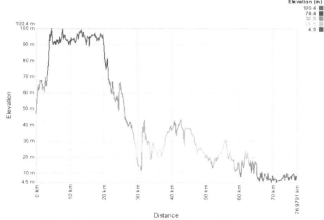

The first half of this section is made up prodominently of canal paths, cycle paths and old tramways whilst the second half is mostly road.

The section starts on the cycleway in Hindley which climbs to the Leeds and Liverpool Canal. The canal tow path is variable and some sections may be very bumpy, although conditions can change considerably over time. The route follows the canal path for ten miles to Whittle le Woods where it picks up the Cuerdon Valley Park Cycle Route to Bamber Bridge.

From Bamber Bridge an Old Tramway leads to Preston, where back roads link to the start of the Lancaster Canal. After only a short distance the canal is left and a variety of small roads and paths lead to the A6 at Broughton.

Just after joining the A6 a cycle lane appears. From this point the road is wide and probably as safe as a major A road can be, most of the traffic using the nearby M6.

The A6 is followed for seven miles until the route bears left before Garstang to follow quieter roads and lanes for a further seven miles. The Lune Estuary Footpath then leads into Lancaster where the route sticks close to the river before climbing to the Lancaster Canal, on top of the Lune Aqueduct, the end of the section.

71

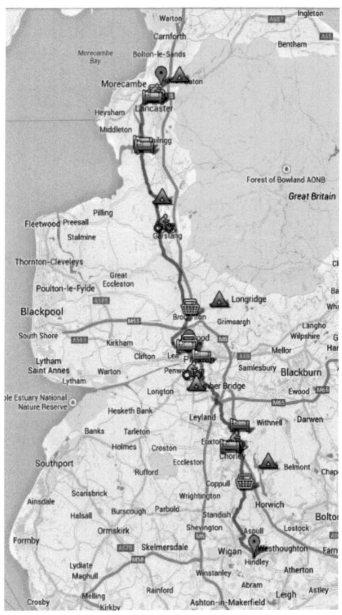

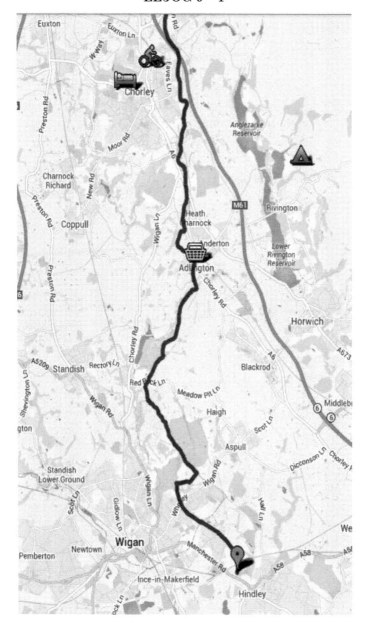

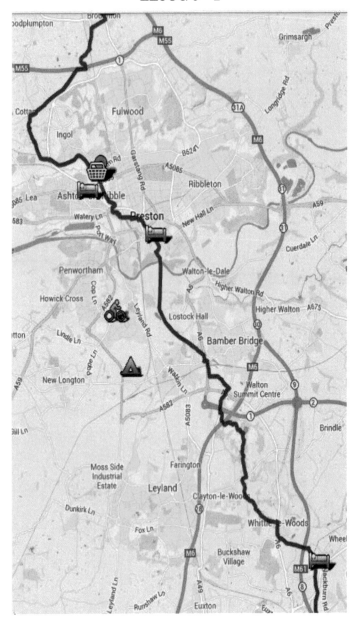

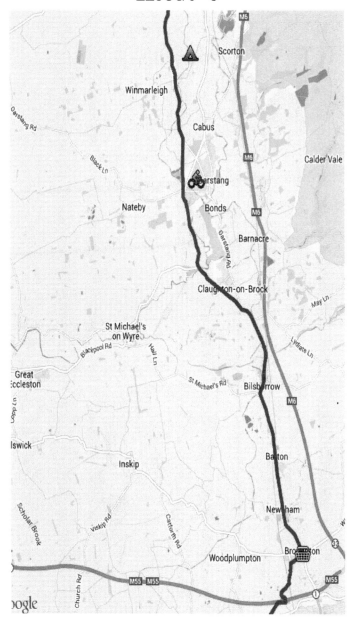

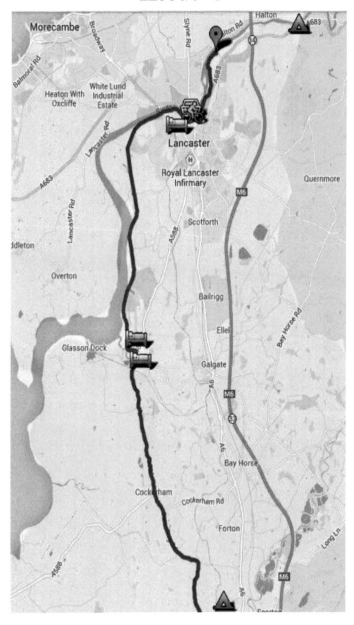

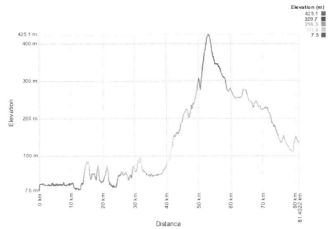

It is clear from the elevation profile that there is a major challenge on this section. The scale will not help this time, it is a major climb, one of the three toughest on the route (the other two being close together at the beginning of the last leg from Helmsdale to John O'Groats – sorry). Arguably this is the hardest.

However, the first 25 miles are easy going. The route starts on the Lancaster Canal, which is followed for seven miles to Carnforth and makes a pleasant start to the section. In Carnforth the route transfers to quiet roads for a further seven miles into Milnthorpe where there is a short but stiff climb. This is the prelude to another eight miles of lanes, with a couple of stiff but short climbs, which lead to Kendal.

The route now follows the A6 for the next twenty four miles, up and over Shap Fell, through the village of Shap and on towards Penrith. The A6 is not busy at this point, all major traffic conveyed on the nearby M6.

The climb to the top of Shap Fell begins shortly after Kendal. The gradient is not extreme but is wearing because it grinds on for mile after mile. There are some sections of about 10%, the most notable being close to the top. The descent towards Penrith is a well earnt reward

77

but is sadly not as long as the ascent and is over far too soon to fully compensate for all that slog upwards. But you can plummet down feeling happy that you have conquered what is probably the hardest climb on the whole route.

Figure 10 - View Climbing Shap Fell

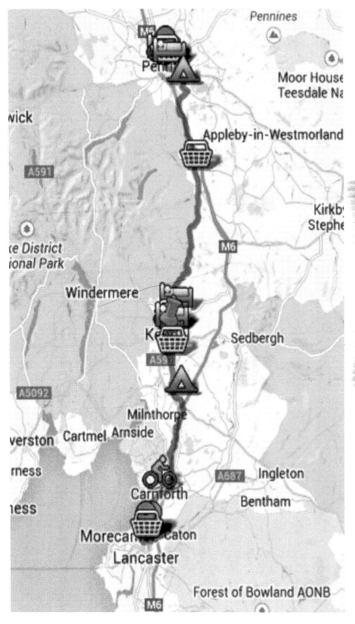

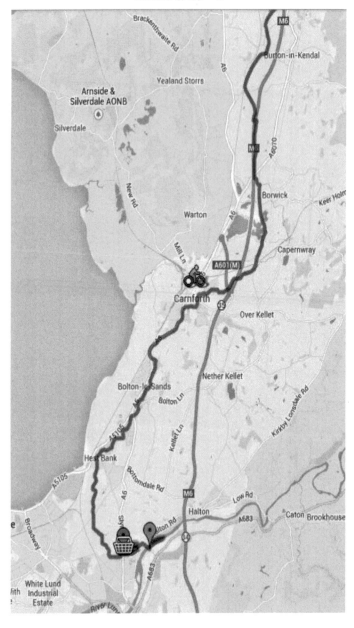

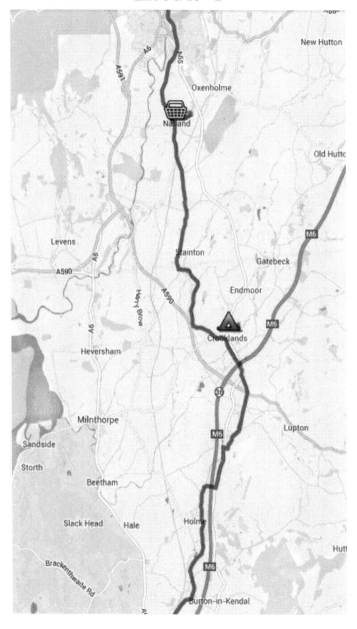

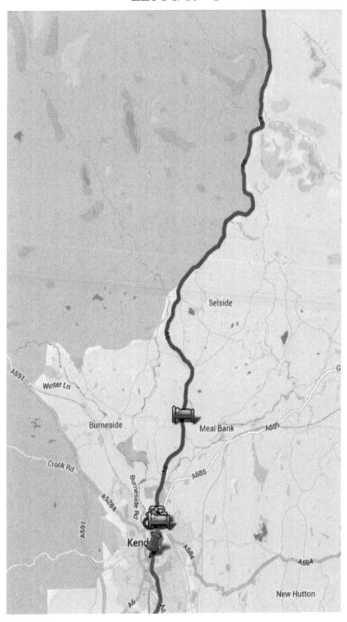

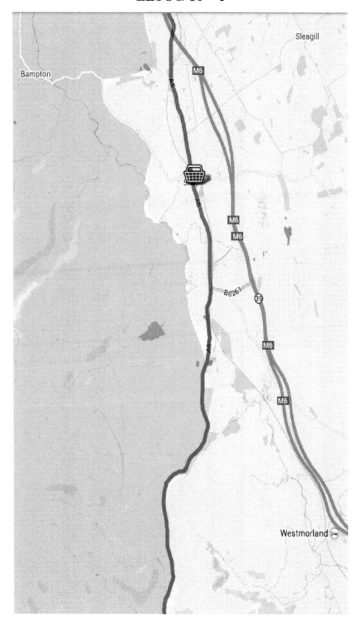

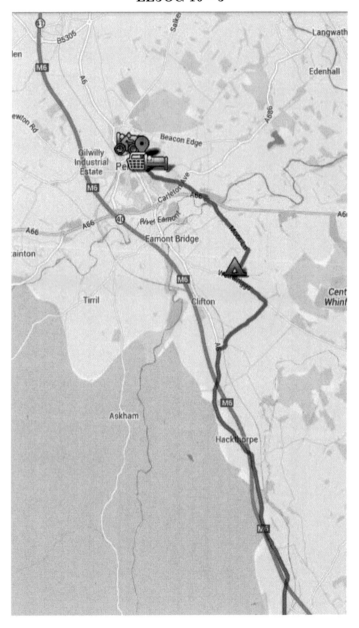

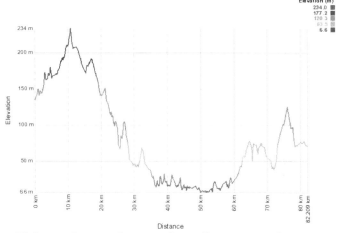

This section marks a major milestone on the route - the crossing of the border from England into Scotland. If the Independence Referendum had swung the other way you might have needed a passport to cross the border but most end to enders still mark the moment with a photo at the (usually defaced) 'Welcome to Sctoland' sign.

The route leaves Penrith on farm lanes before climbing through a farm to join minor roads leading twenty one miles to Carlisle.

Shortly after the village of Skelton the route passes Skelton Radio Mast, the tallest man made structure in the UK. At 365 metres high, it dwarfs the Shard's mere 306 metres.

Approaching Carlisle the road becomes progressively busier up to a right hand turn at traffic lights. After this point there is a cyclepath on the pavement, running past Carlisle Castle.

The route leaves Carlisle almost as soon as it arrives, following minor roads to the border. There is one short stretch of road that is busy but at that point it is wide and straight.

Having crossed the border and sampled the dubious

85

delights of Gretna, the route follows more minor roads north west for seven miles, where it joins the B7076. The B7076 is an excellent road for fast cycling, having steady gradients, generally good surfaces and a cycle lane.

The section ends on the outskirts of Lockerbie, ten miles along the B7076.

Figure 11 - Scottish Border

LEJOG 11 – Whole – Penrith to Lockerbie

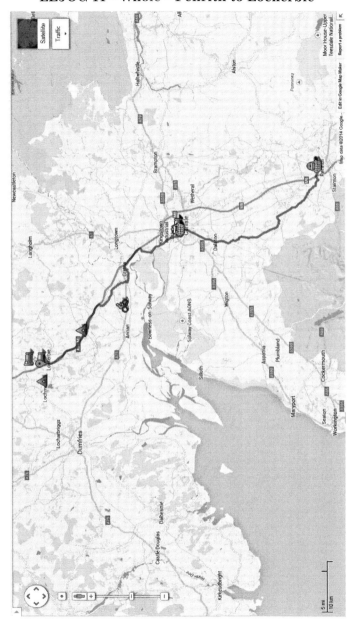

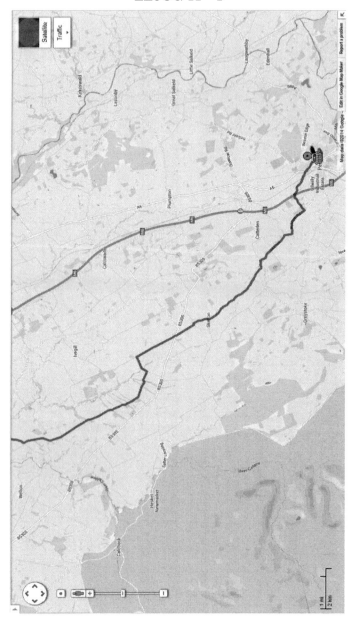

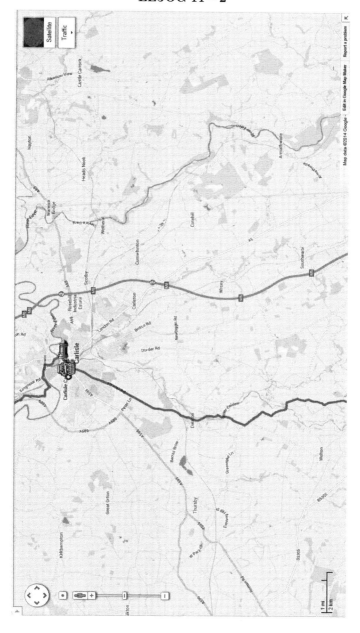

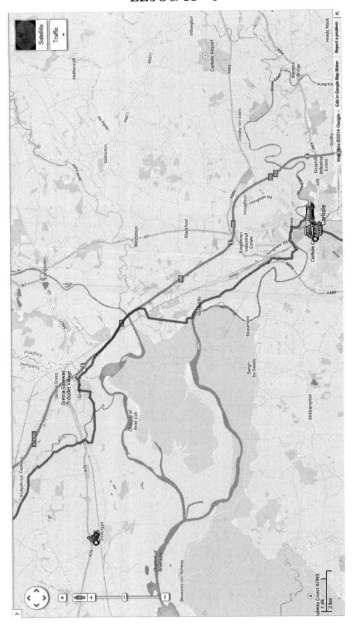

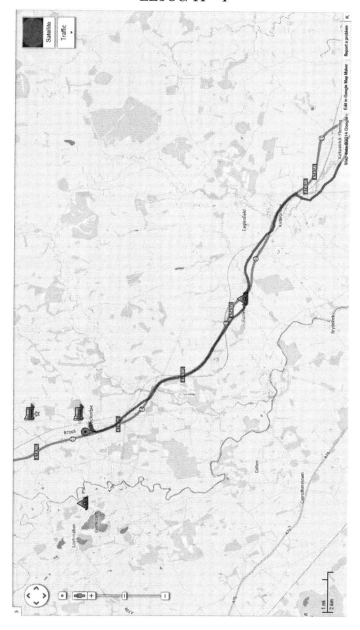

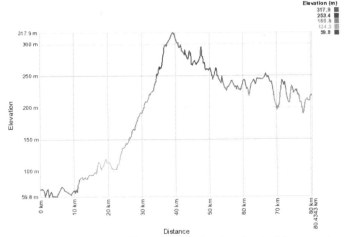

The elevation profile seems to be dominated by a major climb on this section. However the elevation gained is 200 metres over a distance of more than ten miles and is fairly gradual.

The route starts on the B7076 on the outskirts of Lockerbie and continues along the road for twenty eight miles at which point it joins the A702. On the ground the A702 actually seems to join the B7076 at a T junction and if you didn't know you would not notice any change apart from the fact that the cycle lane soon disappears.

The A702 is followed for six miles before turning onto the A73. The A702 has one major roundabout. You can navigate around this on the pavement heading anti clockwise.

The A73 is followed for eight miles before turning onto smaller roads for the last seven miles to the end of the section in Carnwath.

Please note that without detouring into Moffat there is no shop between Lockerbie and the end of the section in Carnwath.

LEJOG 12 – Whole – Lockerbie to Carnwath

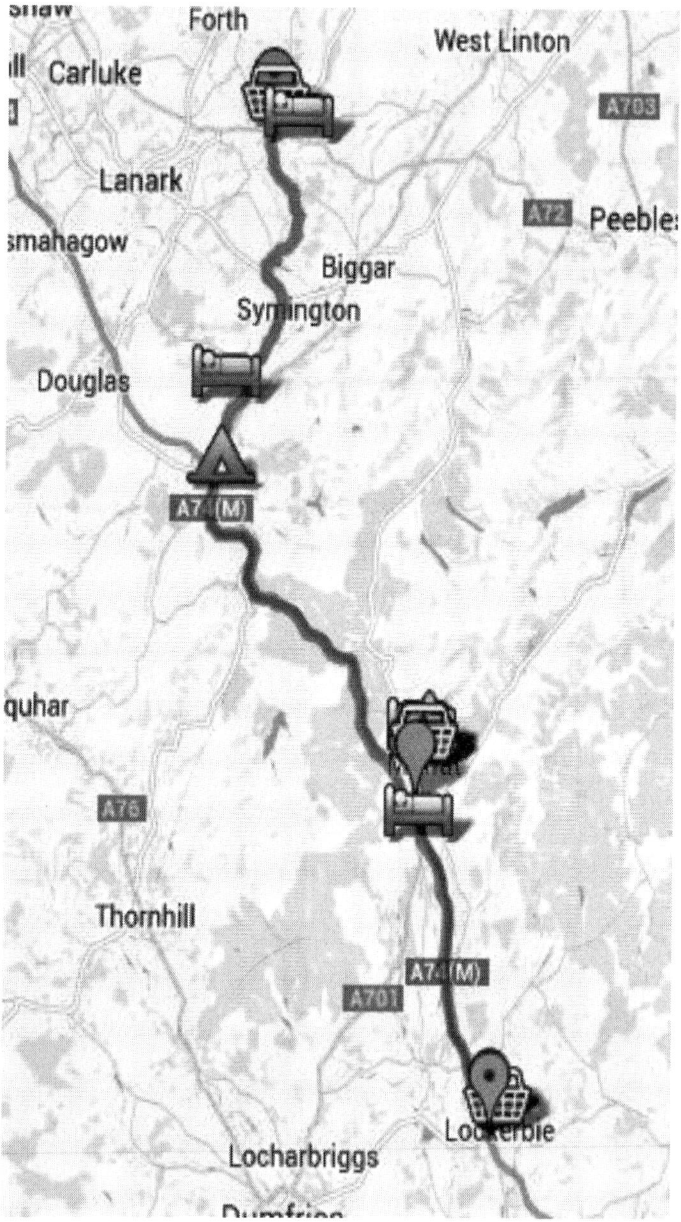

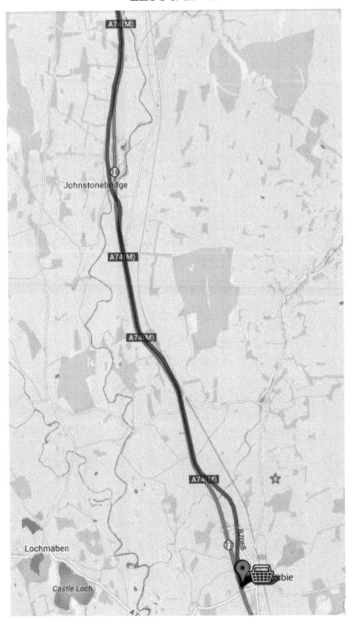

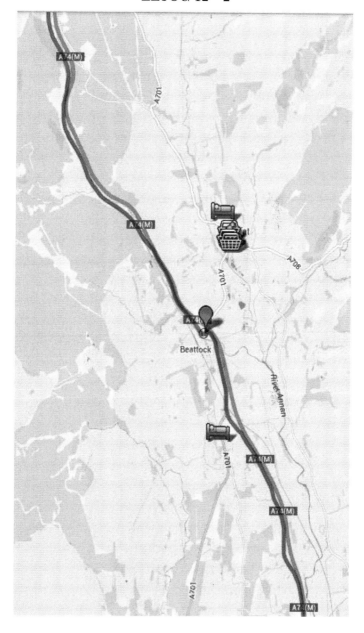

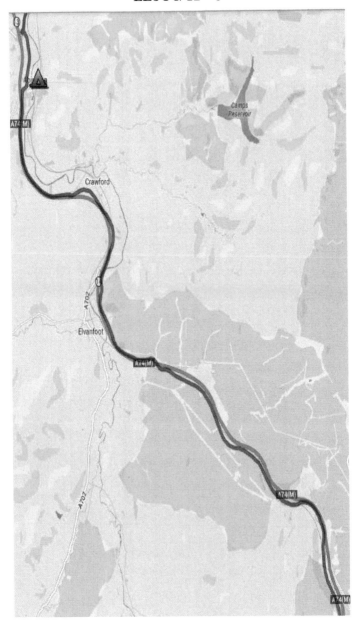

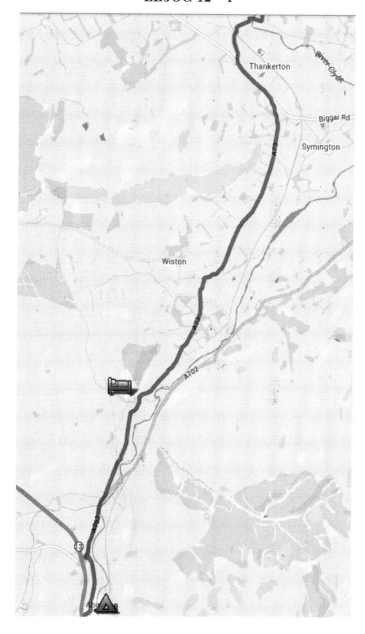

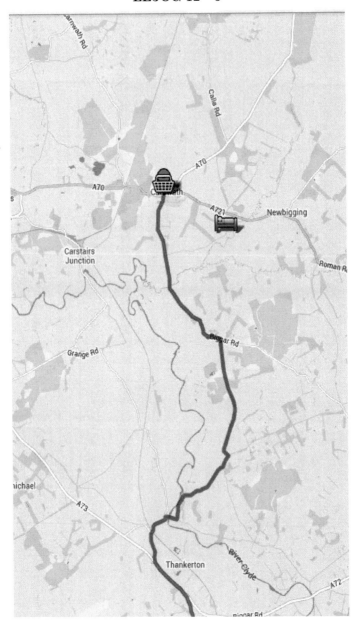

LEJOG 13
Carnwath to Kinross

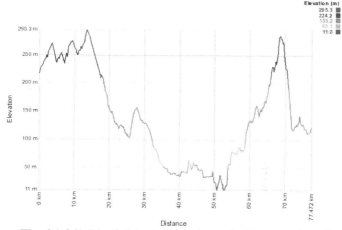

Distance

The highlight of this section is probably crossing the Forth Road Bridge, with views of Queensferry and the iconic Forth Rail Bridge.

From the elevation profile it can be seen that after the first few miles the road tips generally downhill for about twenty five miles to the crossing of the Firth of Forth. Unfortunately it then rears back up to the original elevation but in about one third of the distance, before dumping half of the gain in the next couple of miles.

Leaving Carnwath the route follows the A70 for a mile or so before turning onto minor roads, which it follows for twelve miles to the outskirts of Livingstone.

In Livingstrone the route follows a complex network of paths and back roads before joining the A89.

The A89 is a very busy road but has an excellent cyclepath on a broad pavement counterflowing the traffic. As an added bonus it is downhill. After about four miles the cyclepath crosses to the left. The route continues to follow it for another half mile, over a bridge across the M9.

Following an old tramway and back streets the route heads to the Forth Road Bridge, which is crossed on a cylepath leading into Inverkeithing.

The route then drags upwards through the outskirts of

Dunfermline using back roads and paths. Beyond Dunfermline the road continues to climb, though through a more pleasant landscape. The climb, eventually peaks in the Blairadam Forest before plunging down into Kinross, where the section ends.

Figure 12 - Forth Road Bridge, nr Edinburgh

LEJOG 13 – Whole – Carnwath to Kinross

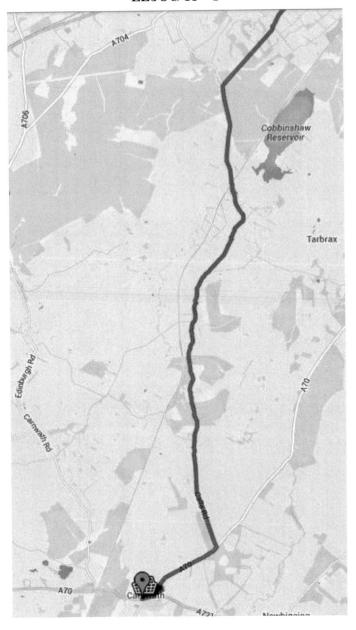

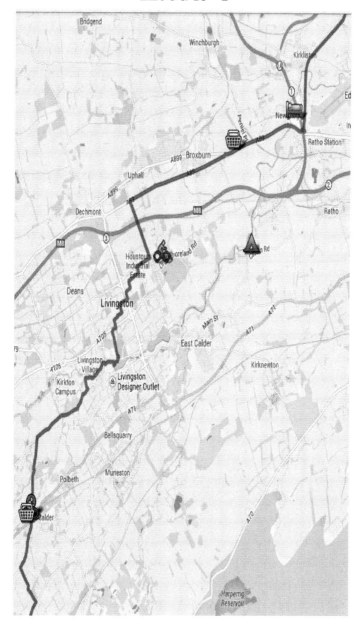

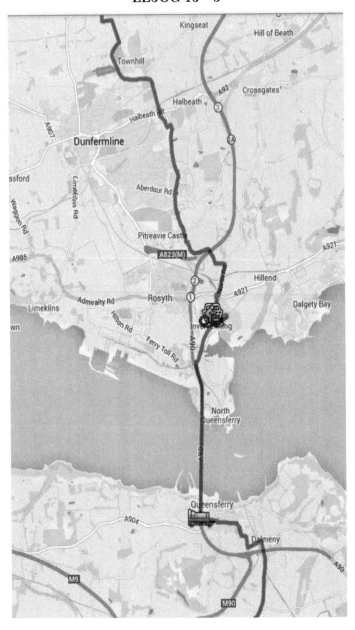

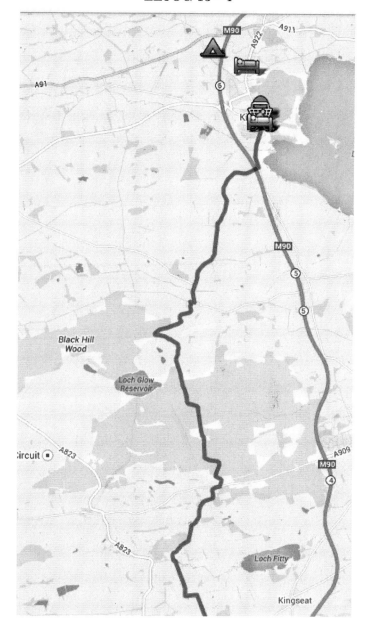

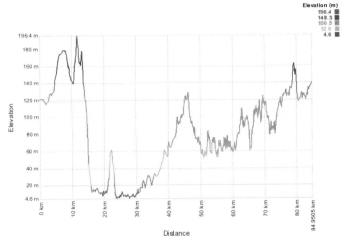

Leaving Kinross the route soon joins minor roads to weave back and forth, over and under the M90 to Perth (not Australia). The elevation shows a notably long and steep descent on which I recorded my highest speed on the entire trip on both of my test rides (about 50mph).

The route leaves Perth on a cylepath along the banks of the River Tay. Thereafter it uses minor roads that shadow the A9 to Dunkeld, a further sixteen miles into the section. Just after Luncarthy there is a short stretch of approximately half a mile on the A9, to link from one minor road to another.

From Dunkeld the route follows an off road track (not very off road) to link with the A9. There is a cyclepath alongside the A9, which is followed for a quarter of a mile to join minor roads once more.

The alternative to using the off road track is to join the A9 before Dunkeld and follow it for two and a half miles to rejoin the route at this point.

The eleven mile stretch into Pitlochry is excellent, infinetely better than following the A9, the way the original route took.

From Pitlochry the route continues to shadow the A9

to the end of the section in Blair Atholl.

Figure 13 - The Tay Viaduct, Logierait nr Pitlochry

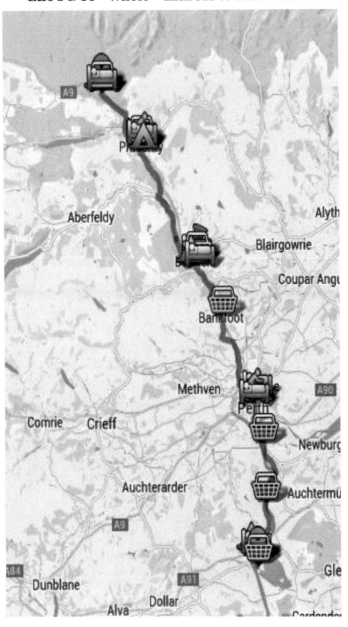

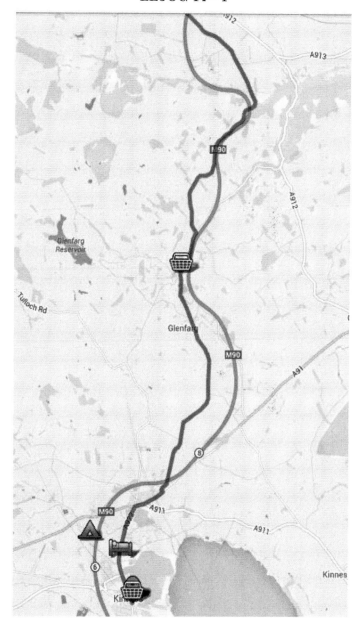

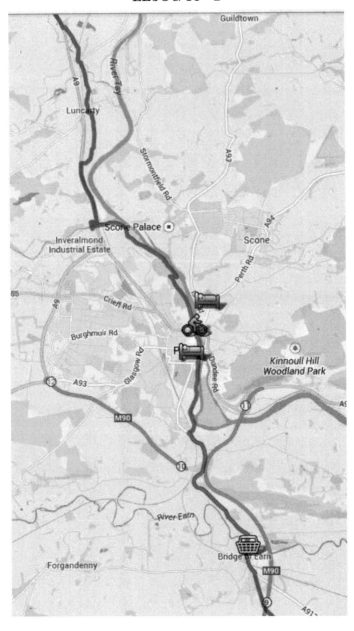

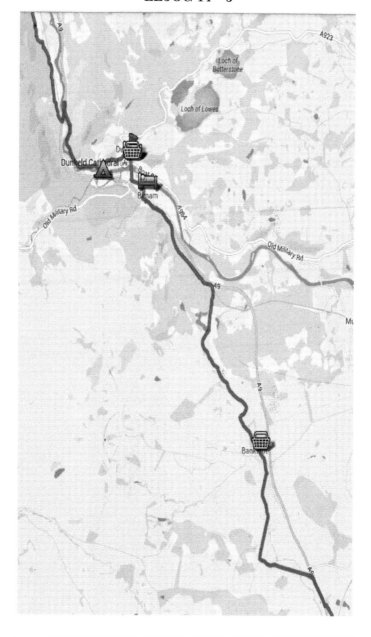

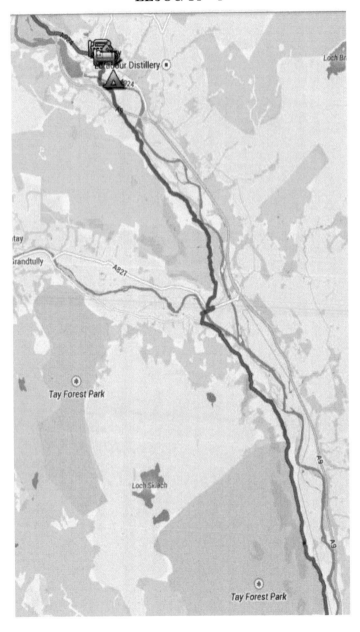

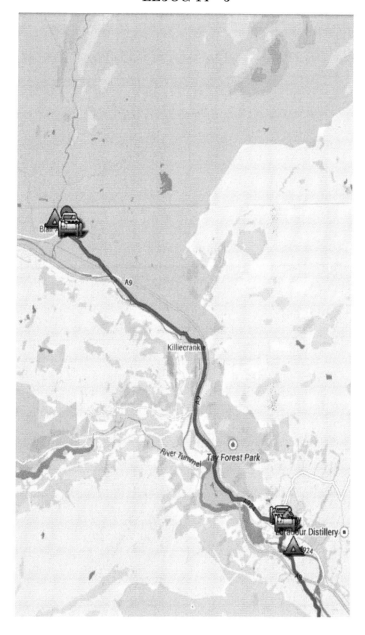

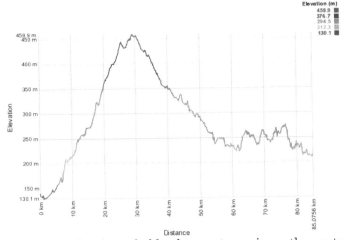

This section is probably the most scenic on the route and has some of the most pleasuarble riding, the former undoubtably having an effect on the latter.

Make sure to top up with drink and food before leaving Blair Atholl because the next shop is thirty five miles further on in Newtonmore.

The route leaves Blair Atholl, continuing along the B847. After four and a half miles it joins a cycleway that shadows the A9 for approximately thirty miles to Newtonmore.

The path climbs gradually up the Drumochter Pass to Drumochter Summit. At 462 metres above sea level this is the highest point on the entire route. Despite being a climb, the fifteen miles or so to the top are some of the best riding on the whole route.

The seventeen miles from the summit to Newtonmore are considerably faster than the similar distance from the start to the top, being mostly downhill.

You will probably need to re-stock in Newtonmore. You will come to a services, a post office and a small supermarket in that order. If you would like to take a break at this point I would recommend cycling on for a further four miles to enjoy the views of Ruthven Barracks.

The fourteen miles from the barracks to Aviemore are, again, some of the best on the route, although Aviemore itself is souless and disappointing.

Figure 14 - Path Climbing Drumochter Pass

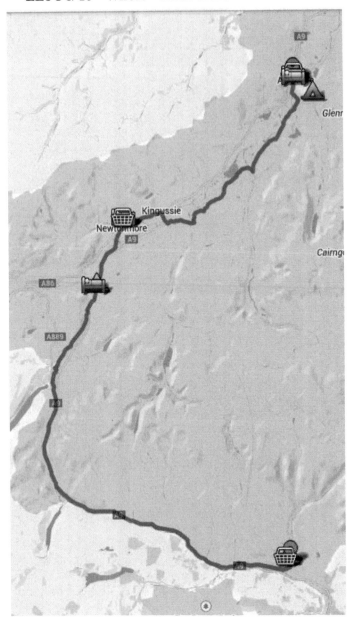

LEJOG 15 – 1

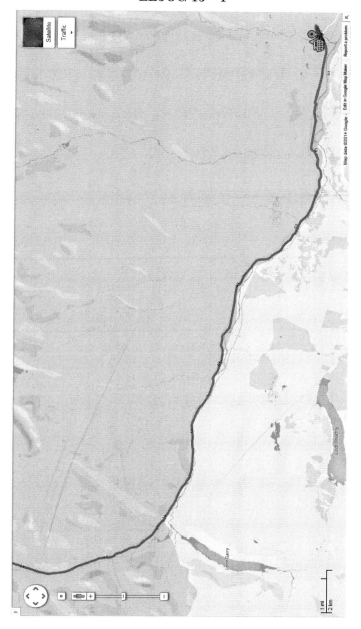

117

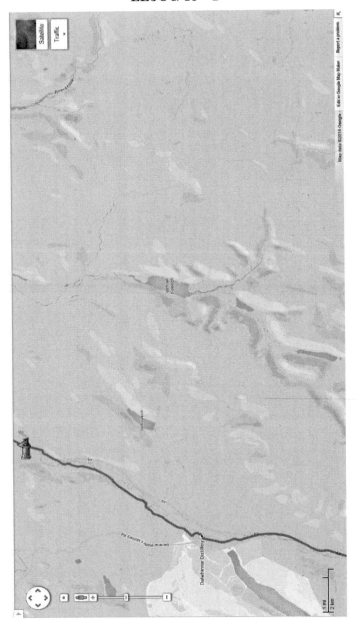

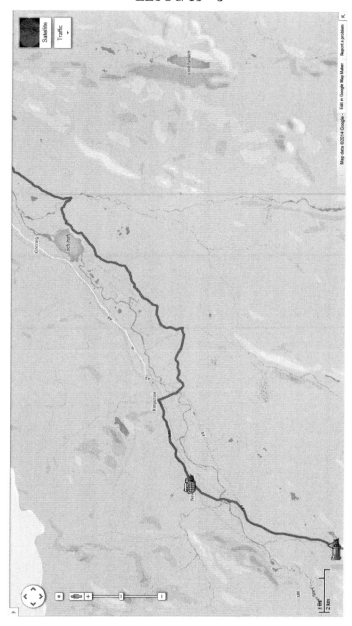

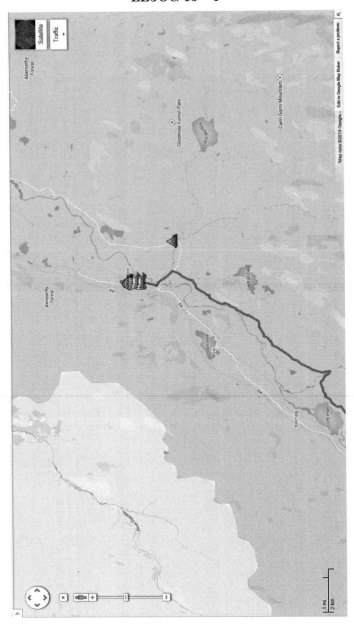

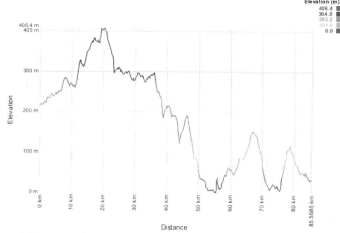

The route follows the B9152 out of Aviemore to join the A95 for two and a half miles before turning back onto the B9152.

In Carrbridge (look out for the ruined bridge on the left) the route turns left onto the A935 and starts the climb towards the Slochd Summit and out of the Cairngorms in earnst.

For the final part of the climb the route joins a cyclepath and continues on it for the start of the descent towards Tomatin.

From Tomatin the general downward gradient continues on minor roads for fourteen miles to the outskirts of Inverness. Here back roads link to the A9 to cross the Kessock Bridge over the Beauly Firth. There is a cyclepath on the pavement.

The route then picks up National Cycle Route 1 and follows it for eighteen miles through Dingwall to the end of the section in Evanton.

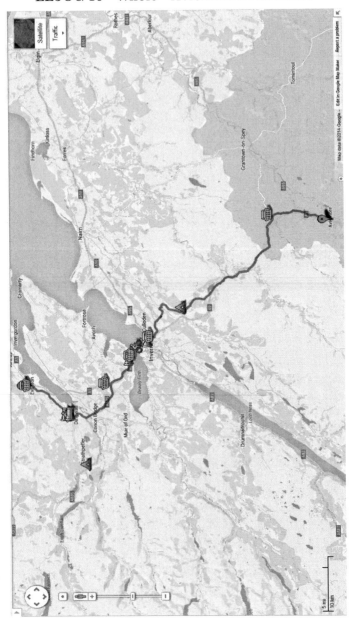

LEJOG 16 – 1

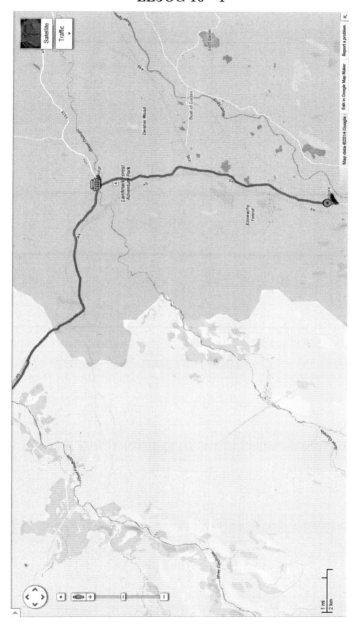

123

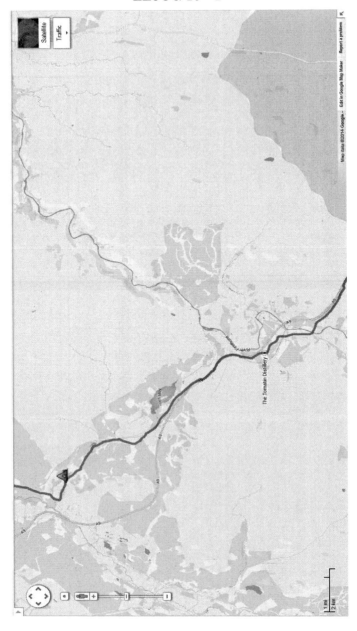

LEJOG 16 – 3

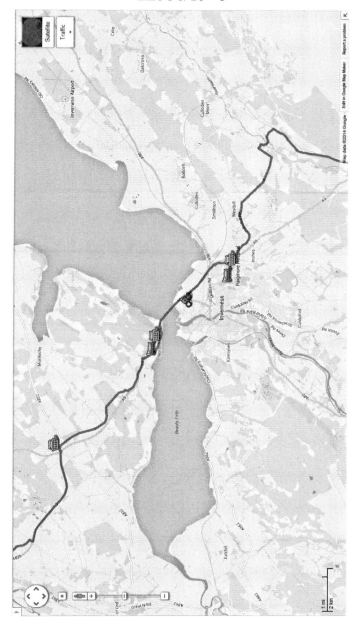

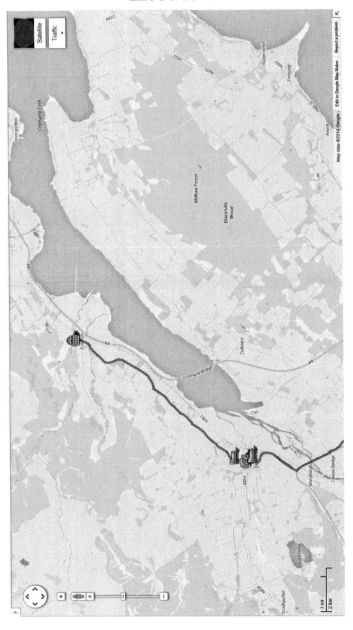

LEJOG 17
Evanton to Helmsdale

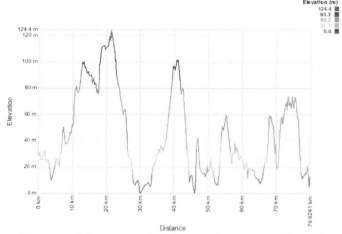

Distance

The penultimate section has a choppy profile with a few stiff climbs, reminiscent of the undulations in Cornwall but on much more open roads. The open roads leave you exposed to the wind but offer fantastic rural and coastal views.

From Evanton the route continues along National Cycle Route 1 for sixteen miles through Alness to join the A9 on the outskirts of Tain.

Just under three miles after joining the A9 it turns right at a roundabout to cross the Dornoch Firth. Here is the first sign on the route for John O'Groats: 85 miles.

The A9 is followed for a further thirty one miles, through Golspie and Brora, to the end of the section in Helmsdale.

On the climb out of Golspie it is worth visiting Dunrobin Castle Railway Station (opposite the entrance to Dunrobin Castle).

This far north the A9 is much quieter than it is up until Inverness and continues to get quieter the further north you cycle.

127

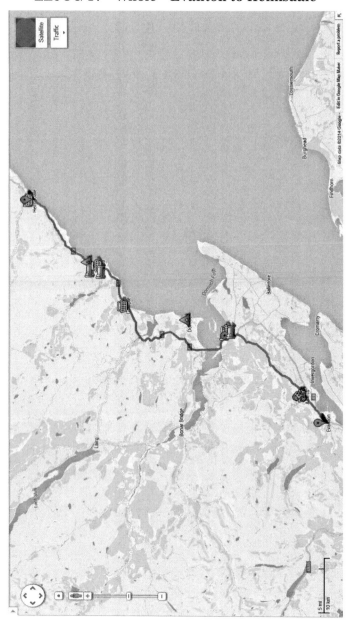

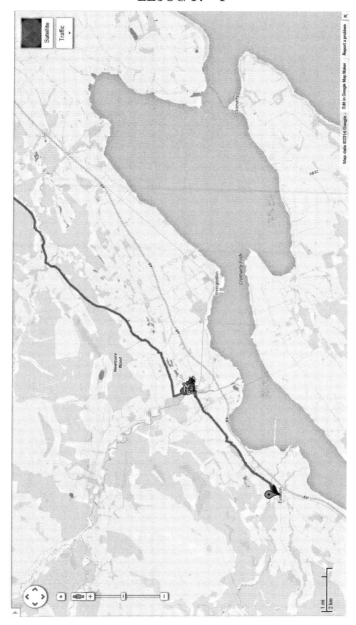

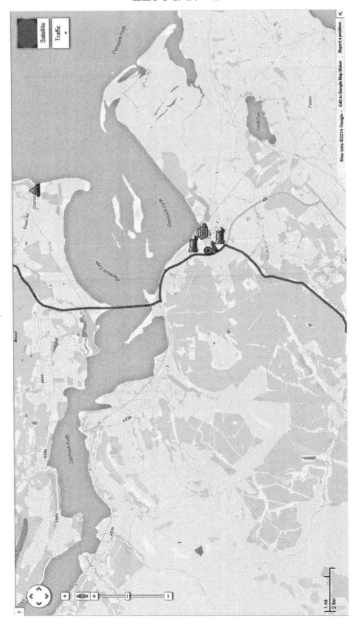

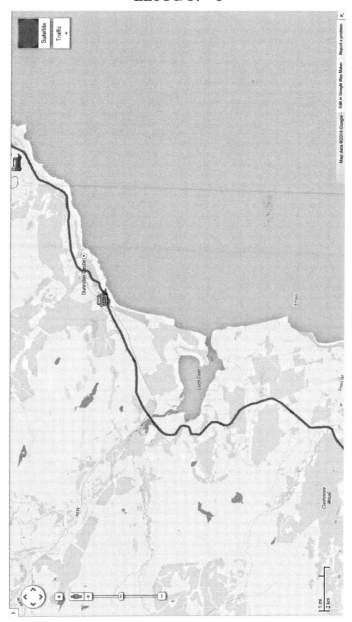

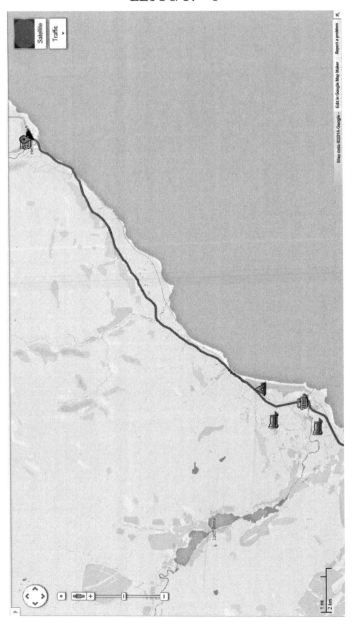

LEJOG 18
Helmsdale to John O'Groats

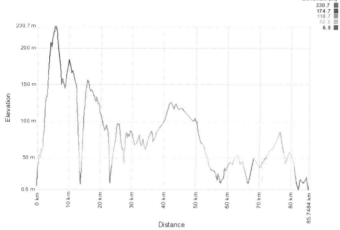

The final section – woo hoo!

The navigation for the first 23 miles is easy – follow the A9 then turn left onto a single track road signed Camster 4.

Unfortunately the riding is more challenging.

The first challenge starts immediately, with a massive climb out of Helmsdale. But before starting up it stock up with drink in Helmsadle. You may not appreciate the extra weight on the climb but the only other shops on the route are in Lybster (a half mile off the route at about twenty two miles) and Watten (thirty six miles).

The Helmsdale climb is shorter than Shap Fell (section 10) but is more relentless and your legs have completed another seven sections since then. You will probably be searching for gears lower than the ones you have.

On reaching the top there is a short descent then the road rises again before plunging at a steep gradient down Berriedale Braes from an elevation of about 170 metres to almost sea level. Here begins the secoind challenge as the road immediately climbs back to a 150 metre elevation in the next mile. This climb is painful coming so soon after the Helmsdale climb.

A few miles on there is a third stiff climb but thankfully it is much shorter. Thereafter the gradient evens out (relatively speaking).

About a mile before the turn off the A9 there is a shop in Lybster. This is found by taking a right turn at the crossroads in Lybster and riding about half a mile into the village.

The turn off the A9 comes immediately after the town sign for Occumster. The road is single track and very straight, leading due north through the Camster Forest. Keep an eye out for the Camster Cairns five miles along the road, on the left.

In Watten (shop) the route then strikes north-north east towards the finish in John O'Groats, eighteen miles distant, using minor roads. Again, some of these roads are very straight, giving the false impression that not much headway is being made. One section of road continues straight for seven miles with just the slight undulation of the road masking sight of road stretching on to the horizon.

The last few miles are generally downhill but the last couple of miles can drag on especially if you are riding into a headwind. However, once you make the final turn onto the main road it is a quarter mile plunge downhill to the signpost and the finish.

Hoorah!!

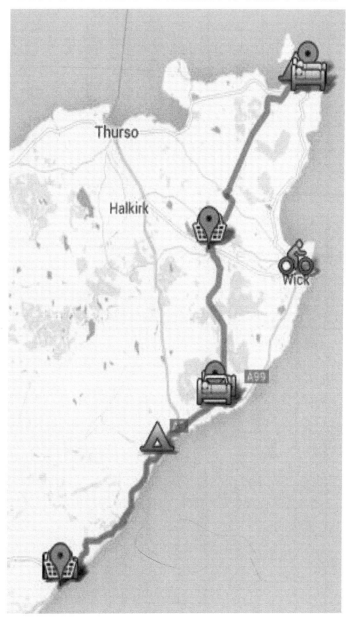

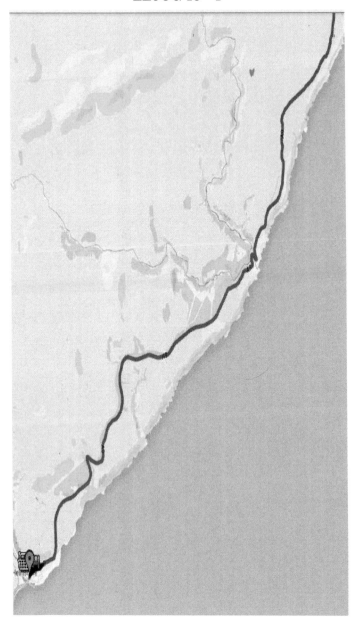

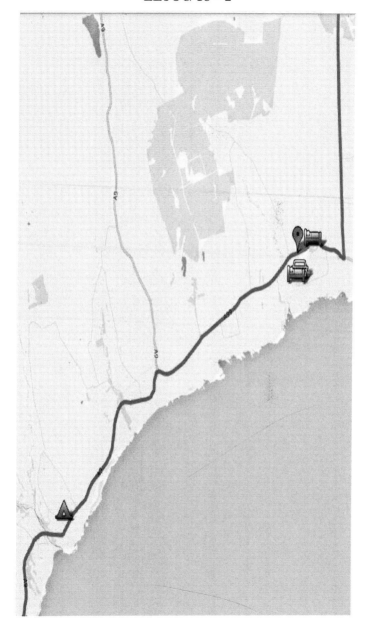

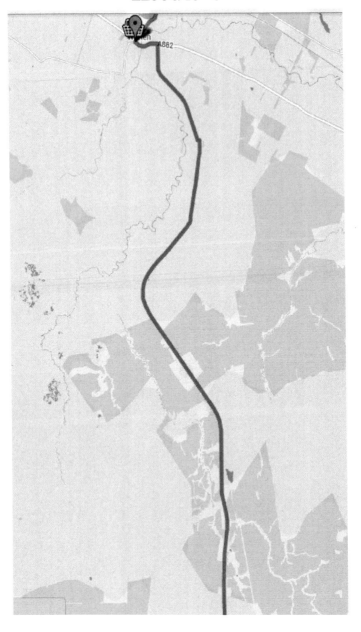

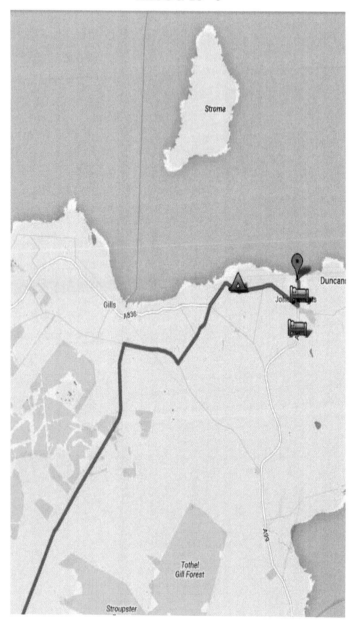

Chapter Four

Accommodation

The following list gives details of accommodation along or within a short cycle of the route. It is not an exhaustive list and in some places there are many more options available. I have selected two B&Bs and one camping site (where available) at approximately 20-25 mile steps along the route. I have included more at Land's End because it is a congestion point.

Please note that unless the accommodation has been reviewed on my website (www.landsend-to-johnogroats.co.uk) then I have no actual knowledge of the accommodation. The accommodation in the list has been selected purely on the following criteria:

1. It is close to the route.
2. It is reasonably priced.
3. It has received descent reviews.
4. It has a website.

In some areas, if availability is thin on the ground, some accommodation listed might not have a website or may not be really close to the route, particularly some of the camping options.

If you use the links to Google Maps (see appendix one) you will see the accommodation on the map. There is a red bed symbol for B&Bs and a green tent symbol for camping. To see which listed accommodation the symbol relates to click on the symbol.

Land's End
B&Bs

The Old Success Inn
Sennen Cove, Cornwall
TR19 7DG, UK
+44 (0)1736 871232
oldsuccess.co.uk

Mayon Farmhouse
Sennen, Cornwall
TR19 7AD, UK
+44 (0)1736 871757
mayonfarmhouse.co.uk

The Land's End Hotel
Land's End, Cornwall
TR19 7AA, UK
+44 (0)1736 871844
landsendhotel.co.uk

Atlantic Lodge
Sunny Corner Lane, Sennen
Cornwall TR19 7AX, UK
+44 (0)1736 871171
atlantic-lodge.co.uk

Whitesands Hotel
Maria's Lane, Sennen
Cornwall, TR19 7AR, UK
+44 (0)1736 871776
whitesandshotel.co.uk

Land's End Hostel
Mill Barn, Land's End
Cornwall TR19 7AQ, UK
+44 (0)7519 309908
landsendhostelaccommodation.co.uk

Campsites

Sennen Cove Camping and Caravanning Club Site
Higher Tregiffian Farm, St Buryan, Penzance, TR19 6JB, UK
+44 (0)1736 871588
campingandcaravanningclub.co.uk

Lower Treave Caravan And Camping Park
Penzance, Cornwall TR19 6HZ, UK
+44 (0)1736 810559
lowertreave.co.uk

Trevedra Farm Caravan & Camping Site
Sennen, Penzance, Cornwall TR19 7BE, UK
+44 (0)1736 871818
trevedrafarm.co.uk

Cardinney Caravan & Camping Park
Crows-an-Wra, St. Buryan, Penzance, TR19 6HX, UK
+44 (0)1736 810880
cardinney-camping-park.co.uk

Penzance
B&Bs

Honeydew Guest House
3 Leskinnick Street
Penzance TR18 2HA, UK
+44 (0)1736 364206
penzance-bed-breakfast.co.uk

Penrose
8 Penrose Terrace
Penzance TR18 2HQ, UK
+44 (0)1736 362782
bandbinpenzance.com

Campsites

Wild Camping
4 Beacon Estate
Sancreed, Penzance TR20 8QR, UK
+44 (0)7776 223337
wildcampingcornwall.co.uk

Camborne
B&Bs

Bikers B&B
Palm Springs, 38 New Rd
Barripper, Camborne
Cornwall TR14 0QS, UK
+44 (0)1209 719145
bikers-bed-and-breakfast.com

Cherry Villa B & B
21 Trevu Road
Camborne, Cornwall TR14
7AE, UK
+44 (0)1209 610135
cherryvillacornwall.com

Campsites

Lavender Fields Touring Park
Lavender Fields
Penhale Road, Carnhell Green, Carnhell Green, Cornwall
TR14 0LU, UK
+44 (0)1209 832188
lavenderfieldstouring.co.uk

Wheal Rose Caravan & Camping Park
Wheal Rose
Scorrier, Redruth TR16 5DD, UK
+44 (0)1209 891496
whealrosecaravanpark.co.uk

St Newlyn East
B&Bs

Chy-An-Eglos B & B
5 Churchtown, St Newlyn East
Newquay, Cornwall TR8 5LQ
+44 (0)1872 519270
chy-an-eglos-bb.co.uk

Degembris Manor Farm
St Newlyn East, Newquay
TR8 5HY, UK
+44 (0)1872 510555
degembris.co.uk

Campsites

Trethiggey Holiday Park
Little Trethiggey, Newquay, Cornwall TR8 4QR, UK
+44 (0)1637 877672
trethiggey.co.uk

Bodmin
B&Bs

Butterwell Fishery
Nanstallon, Bodmin, Cornwall
PL30 5LQ, UK
+44 (0)1208 831515
butterwellfishery.co.uk

South Tregleath Farm
Washaway
Bodmin PL30 3AA, UK
+44 (0)1208 72692
south-tregleath.co.uk

Campsites

Ruthern Valley Holidays
Ruthernbridge, Bodmin, Cornwall PL30 5LU, UK
+44 (0)1208 831395
ruthernvalley.com

Holsworthy
B&Bs

Oak Tree Farm. B&B
Burnards House, Holsworthy
Devon EX22 7JA, UK
+44 (0)1409 254870
bandbinholsworthy.co.uk

Thorne Park
Chilsworthy, Holsworthy
Devon EX22 7BL, UK
+44 (0)1409 253339
thornepark-devon.co.uk

Campsites

Tamarstone Farm
Pancrasweek, Holsworthy EX22 7JT, UK
+44 (0)1288 381734
tamarstone.co.uk

Hatherleigh
B&Bs

Nichols Nymet House
North Tawton, Devon
EX20 2BP
UK
+44 (0)1837 82626
devonbedandbreakfast.co.uk

Weirford House
Sampford Courtenay
Okehampton, Devon
EX20 2SY   UK
+44 (0)1837 89132
weirfordhouse.co.uk

Campsites

Legge Farm
Church Rd, Highampton, Beaworthy, Devon EX21 5LF, UK
+44 (0)1409 231464
leggefarm.co.uk

Tiverton
B&Bs

Bridge Guest House
23 Angel Hill
Tiverton
EX16 6PE
UK
+44 (0)1884 252804

Angel
13 Saint Peter Street
Tiverton, Devon
EX16 6NU, UK
+44 (0)1884 253392
angelguesthouse.co.uk

Campsites

Minnows Touring Park
Sampford Peverell, Tiverton, Devon EX16 7EN, UK
+44 (0)1884 821770
ukparks.co.uk

Taunton
B&Bs

The Old Mill
Netherclay
Bishop's Hull, Taunton
Somerset TA1 5AB, UK
+44 (0)1823 289732
bandbtaunton.co.uk

Lowdens House
26 Wellington Road
Taunton, Somerset
TA1 4EQ, UK
+44 (0)1823 336586
tauntonguesthouse.co.uk

Campsites

Ashe Farm Caravan & Camping Site
Thornfalcon, Taunton TA3 5NW, UK
+44 (0)1823 443764
ashefarm.co.uk

Cheddar
B&Bs

Notlake Farm B&B
Lower Notlake Drove
Clewer, Wedmore Nr Cheddar
Somerset BS28 4JW, UK
+44 (0)1934 742096
notlakefarmbedandbreakfast.co.uk

Strawberry Line B&B
Chilfurlong House
Cheddar Road, Axbridge,
Somerset, BS26 2DL, UK
+44 (0)1934 732573
strawberrylinebedandbreakfast.co.uk

Campsites

Petruth Paddocks Ltd
Labourham Drove
Cheddar, Somerset BS27 3XW, UK
+44 (0)7813 320870
petruthpaddocks.co.uk

Clevedon
B&Bs

Elm Tree Cottage Hotel
Jacklands Bridge, Tickenham
Nailsea, North Somerset
BS21 6SQ, UK
+44 (0)1275 866484
a-specialplacetostay.co.uk

Cavell House
1 Elton Road
Clevedon, North Somerset
BS21 7RA, UK
+44 (0)1275 874477
cavellhouse.com

Campsites

Cranmoor Campsite
Bullocks Lane, Clevedon BS21 6XA, UK
+44 (0)1934 838397
cranmoorcampsite.co.uk

Thornbury
B&Bs

Redhill Farmhouse
Redhill Farmhouse
Olveston, Bristol
BS35 4AG, UK
+44 (0)1454 416773
redhillfarmhouse.co.uk

Oldbury Naite Villa
Oldbury Naite
Oldbury-on-Severn
South Glos. BS35 1RU, UK
+44 (0)1454 414167
naitevilla.co.uk

Campsites

Tudor Caravan Park
Shepherds Patch
Slimbridge, Gloucester GL2 7BP, UK
+44 (0)1453 890483
tudorcaravanpark.com

Gloucester
B&Bs

Spalite Hotel
121 Southgate Street
Gloucester GL1 1XQ, UK
+44 (0)1452 380828
spalitehotel.com

Lulworth Guest House
12 Midland Road
Gloucester GL1 4UF, UK
+44 (0)1452 521881

Campsites

Stone End House Farm
Stone End House Farm
Church Lane, Corse, Gloucester GL19 3BX, UK
+44 (0)1452 700254
stone-end-camping.co.uk

Tewksbury
B&Bs

Willow Cottages B&B
Shuthonger
Gloucestershire GL20 6ED
UK
+44 (0)1684 298599
tewkesburybedandbreakfast.co.uk

Nursery Court B&B
Mythe Road, Tewkesbury,
Gloucestershire GL20 6EB
UK
+44 (0)1684 296963
nurserycourtbandb.co.uk

Campsites

The Willows
Lower Lode, Forthampton, Tewkesbury, Gloucestershire,
England, GL19 4RE, UK
+44 (0)1684 296288
thewillowscaravanpark.co.uk

Worcester
B&Bs

Manor Coach House
Hindlip Lane
Hindlip, Worcester
WR3 8SJ, UK
+44 (0)1905 456457
manorcoachhouse.co.uk

Heathside Guesthouse
172 Droitwich Road
Fernhill Heath, Worcestershire
WR3 7UA
+44 (0)1905 458245
heathsideguesthouse.co.uk

Campsites

Mill House Caravan & Camping Site
Hawford, Worcester WR3 7SE, UK
+44 (0)1905 451283
millhousecaravanandcamping.co.uk

Kidderminster
B&Bs

Premier Inn Kidderminster Hotel
Slingfield Mill
Weavers Wharf, Kidderminster
DY11 6YR, UK
+44 (0)871 527 9350
premierinn.com

Drakelow Manor Guest House
Sladd Lane, Cookley
Kidderminster, Bewdley
Worcestershire DY11 5TF, UK
+44 (0)1562 850920
drakelowmanor.co.uk

Campsites

Wolverley Camping and Caravanning Club Site
Brown Westhead Park
Wolverley, Kidderminster DY10 3PX, UK
+44 (0)1562 850909
campingandcaravanningclub.co.uk

Stafford
B&Bs

Wyndale Guest House
199 Corporation Street
Stafford ST16 3LQ, UK
+44 (0)1785 223069
wyndaleguesthouse.co.uk

Leonards Croft
80 Lichfield Road
Stafford ST17 4LP, UK
+44 (0)1785 223676
leonardscroft.co.uk

Campsites

Pillaton Hall Farm
Pillaton, Penkridge, Stafford ST19 5RZ, UK
+44 (0)1785 715177
pillatonpools.co.uk

Stoke-on-Trent
B&Bs

Kenwood Guest House
14 Shelton, Stoke-on-Trent
ST4 2DP, UK
+44 (0)1782 765787
kenwoodguesthousestoke.co.uk

The Corrie Guest House
13 Newton Street
Stoke on Trent, ST4 6JN
UK
+44 (0)1782 614838

Campsites

Lakeside Tavern
Meaford Road, Nr Barlaston, Stone, Staffordshire ST15 8UX, UK
+44 (0)1782 373242

Lower Withington
B&Bs

Chapel Cottage B&B
Salters Lane
Lower Withington, Cheshire
SK11 9EA, UK
+44 (0)1477 571489
chapelcottage.net

Bridge Farm
Bridge Lane
Holmes Chapel, Crewe
CW4 8BX, UK
+44 (0)1477 571202
bridgefarm.com

Campsites

Manchester
B&Bs

Town Hall Hotel
106 Church Street, Eccles
Manchester M30 0LH, UK
+44 (0)161 707 8978

Woodstock
564-566 Wilbraham Road
Manchester M21 9LB, UK
+44 (0)1622 727900

Campsites

Chorley
B&Bs

Inglewood Boutique B&B
19 Southport Road
Chorley PR7 1LB, UK
+44 (0)7792 957168

Premier Travel Inn
Malthouse Farm, Moss Lane
Chorley PR6 8AB, UK
+44 (0)871 527 8916
premierinn.com

Campsites
Wilcocks Farm Caravan Site
Dean Head Lane, Rivington, Bolton BL6 7SJ, UK
+44 (0)1204 697339
wilcocksfarmcaravansite.co.uk

Preston
B&Bs

The Chaddock Ltd
49 Chaddock Street
Preston, Lancashire PR1 3TL,
UK
+44 (0)1772 251530

Ashton Lodge Guest House
37 Victoria Parade, Preston,
Lancashire PR2 1DT, UK
+44 (0)1772 728414
ashtonlodgepreston.co.uk

Campsites
Stoneycroft
28 Chain House Lane, Preston PR4 4LE, UK
+44 (0)1772 335879
stoneycroftcaravans.co.uk

Whittingham & Goosnargh Sports & Social Club
Whittingham, PR3 2JE, UK
+44 (0)1772 865339
whittinghamclub.com

150

Condor Green
B&Bs

The Stork Inn
Corricks Lane, Conder Green,
Lancaster LA2 0AN, UK
+44 (0)1524 751234
thestorkinn.co.uk

The Mill at Conder Green
Conder Green, Lancaster
LA2 0BD, UK
+44 (0)1524 752852
themillatcondergreen.co.uk

Campsites
Greaves Farm Caravan and Camping Sitemore info
Cabus Nook Lane, Garstang, Lancashire PR3 1AA, UK
+44 (0)1524 791726
greavesfarmcabuscaravansite.co.uk

Lancaster
B&Bs

Lancaster Town House
11-12 Newton Terrace, Caton
Road, Lancaster, LA1 3PB, UK
+44 (0)1524 65527
lancastertownhouse.co.uk

Old Station House B&B
25 Meeting House Lane
Lancaster LA1 1TX, UK
+44 (0)1524 381060
oldstationhouse.info

Campsites
New Parkside Farm
Denny Beck, Lancaster, Lancashire, England, LA2 9HH, UK
+44 (0)1524 770723
newparksidefarm.co.uk

Kendal
B&Bs

Redhills Guest House
Shap Rd, Kendal
Cumbria LA9 6NX, UK
+44 (0)1539 724447

Badger Close B&B
26 Castle Street, Kendal
Cumbria LA9 7AS, UK
+44 (0)1539 726551
badgerclose.co.uk

Campsites
Waters Edge
Crooklands, Cumberia LA7 7NN, UK
+44 (0)15395 67708
watersedgecaravanpark.co.uk

Penrith
B&Bs

Makalolo
Barco Avenue, Penrith
CA11 8LU UK
+44 (0)1768 891519
makalologuesthousepenrith.co.uk

Brooklands guest house
2 Portland Place, Penrith
CA11 7QN, UK
+44 (0)1768 863395
brooklandsguesthouse.com

Campsites

Crossfells Campsite
Clifton Dykes, Penrith, Cumbria CA10 2DG, UK
+44 (0)7551 339697
crossfells-campsite.co.uk

Carlisle
B&Bs

Ashleigh House
12 A6, Carlisle, Cumbria
CA12 1EX, UK
+44 (0)1228 521631
ashleighbedandbreakfast.co.uk

Brooklyn House
42 Victoria Place, Carlisle
Cumbria CA1 1EX, UK
+44 (0)1228 590002
brooklynhouse.co.uk

Campsites

Lockerbie
B&Bs

Bishopcleugh Guest House
Lockerbie
DG11 2RH, UK
+44 (0)1576 203652
bishopcleugh.co.uk

Corrie Lodge Country House B&B
Corrie Road
Lockerbie, DG11 2NG, UK
+44 (0)1576 710237
corrielodgecountryhouse.co.uk

Campsites

Halleaths Caravan Park
Lockerbie, Dumfriesshire, Lockerbie DG11 1NA, UK
+44 (0)1387 810630
halleaths.co.uk

Cressfield Park
Townfoot, Lockerbie, Dumfriesshire DG11 3DR, UK
+44 (0)1576 300702
cressfieldpark.com

Moffat
B&Bs

Marchbankwood House
Beattock, Moffat
Dumfriesshire DG10 9RG, UK
+44 (0)1683 030118
marchbankwood.co.uk

Dell-mar B&B
6 Beechgrove, Moffat
Dumfriesshire, DG10 9RS, UK
+44 (0)1683 220260
dell-mar.co.uk

Campsites
Mount View Caravan Park
Abington, Lanarkshire, Scotland, ML12 6RW, UK
+44 (0)1864 502808
mountviewcaravanpark.co.uk

Carnworth
B&Bs

Roberton B & B
Rosebank Cottage Howgate Rd
Roberton, Biggar, South
Lanarkshire, ML12 6RS, UK
+44 (0)1899 850667
robertonbnb.eu.pn

The Lint Mill B&B
Carnwath
South Lanarkshire
ML11 8LY, UK
+44 (0)1555 840042
thelintmill.co.uk

Campsites

Edinburgh
B&Bs

Premier Inn Edinburgh Airport (Newbridge) Hotel
5 Hallbarns Crescent
Newbridge, Edinburgh
EH28 8TH, UK
+44 (0)871 527 9284
premierinn.com

Premier Inn Edinburgh (South Queensferry) Hotel
Builyeon Road
Queensferry, Edinburgh
EH30 9YJ, UK
+44 871 527 8364
premierinn.com

Campsites

Linwater Caravan Park
Clifton Road, East Calder, West Lothian EH53 0HT, UK
+44 (0)131 333 3326
linwater.co.uk

Kinross
B&Bs

Burnbank B&B
79 Muirs, Kinross
KY13 8AZ, UK
+44 (0)1577 861931
burnbank-kinross.co.uk

Roxburghe Guest House
126 High Street, Kinross
KY13 8AN, UK
+44 (0)1577 864521
roxburgheguesthouse.co.uk

Campsites

Gallowhill Farm
Kinross KY13 0RD, UK
+44 (0)1577 862364
jpaterson21@hotmail.com

Perth
B&Bs

Kinnaird Guest House
5 Marshall Place
Perth PH2 8AH, UK
+44 (0)1738 628021
kinnaird-guesthouse.co.uk

Ballabeg Guest House
14 Keir Street
Perth PH2 7HJ, UK
+44 (0)1738 620434
ballabegguesthouse.co.uk

Campsites

Dunkeld
B&Bs

The Pend
5 Brae St
Dunkeld PH8 0BA, UK
+44 (0)1350 727586
thepend.com

Birnam Guest House
4 Murthly Terrace, Birnam
Dunkeld, PH8 0BG, UK
+44 (0)1350 727201
birnamguesthouse.co.uk

Campsites

Inver Mill Farm Caravan Park
Dunkeld, Perthshire PH8 0JR, UK
+44 (0)1350 727477
invermillfarm.com

Pitlochry
B&Bs

Woodburn B&B
Ferry Road, Pitlochry
Perthshire PH16 5DD, UK
+44 (0)1796 473818
woodburnhouse.co.uk

Bridge House B&B
53 Atholl Road, Pitlochry
Perthshire PH16 5BL, UK
+44 (0)7754 418369
pitlochrybandb.com

Campsites

Milton Of Fonab Caravan Park
Pitlochry, Perthshire PH16 5NA, UK
+44 (0)1796 472882
fonab.co.uk

Blair Atholl
B&Bs

Dalgreine
Off St Andrews Crescent,
Blair Atholl, Perthshire
PH18 5SX, UK
+44 (0)1796 481276
dalgreineguesthouse.co.uk

The Firs Guesthouse
Saint Andrew's Crescent
Blair Atholl, Perthshire
PH18 5SX, UK
+44 (0)1796 481256
firs-blairatholl.co.uk

Campsites

Blair Castle Caravan Park
Blair Atholl, Perthshire & Kinross PH18 5SR, UK
+44 (0)1796 481263
blaircastlecaravanpark.co.uk

Newtonmore
B&Bs

Crubenbeg House
Falls Of Truim
Newtonmore, Inverness-Shire
PH20 1BE, UK
+44 (0)1540 673300
crubenbeghouse.com

B&B Newtonmore
Greenways, Golf Course Road
Newtonmore, Inverness-Shire
PH20 1AT, UK
+44 (0)1540 670136
bedandbreakfastnewtonmore.com

Campsites

Invernahavon
Glentrum, Newtonmore PH20 1BE, UK
+44 (0)1540 673534

Aviemore
B&Bs

Ardlogie Guest House
Dalfaber Road, Aviemore
Inverness-shire
H22 1PU, UK
+44 (0)1479 810747
ardlogie.co.uk

Speybank B&B
Dalfaber Road, Aviemore,
Inverness-shire
PH22 1PU, UK
+44 (0)1479 810055
speybank.com

Campsites

Rothiemurchus Camp & Caravan Park
Coylumbridge, Aviemore, Inverness-shire PH22 1QU, UK
+44 (0)1479 812800
campandcaravan.com

Inverness
B&Bs

Alba Guest House
14 Culcabock Road
Inverness,
IV2 3XQ, UK
+44 (0)1463 230269
alba-inverness.co.uk

Mount Pleasant B&B
16 Marine Park,
North Kessock, Inverness
IV1 3XS, UK
+44 (0)1463 731474
mountpleasant-bedandbreakfast.com

Campsites

Auchnahillin Holiday Park
Daviot, Aberdeenshire, IV2 5XQ, UK
+44 (0)1463 772286
auchnahillin.co.uk

Dingwell
B&Bs

Marsule B&B
Craig Road, Dingwall
Ross-Shire IV15 9LF, UK
+44 (0)1349 862201
marsule.co.uk

Dingwall B&B
4 Hill Street, Dingwall
Ross-Shire IV15 9JP, UK
+44 (0)7841 403646
dingwallbedandbreakfast.co.uk

Campsites

Riverside Chalets and Caravan Park
Contin, Strathpeffer, Highlands IV14 9ES, UK
+44 (0)1463 513599
lochness-chalets.co.uk

Tain
B&Bs

Rosslyn B&B
4 Hartfield Gardens
Tain, IV19 1DL, UK
+44 (0)1862 892697
rosslyntain.co.uk

Morangie B&B
2 Morangie Road
Tain IV19 1PY, UK
+44 (0)1862 893855
morangiebandb.com

Campsites

Dornoch Camping & Caravan Site
The Links, Dornoch, Sutherland IV25 3LX, UK
+44 (0)1862 810423
dornochcaravans.co.uk

Brora
B&Bs

Inverbrora Farm B&B
Brora, Sutherland
KW9 6NJ, UK
+44 (0)1408 621208
inverbrora.com

Clynelish Farm B&B
Clynelish, Brora, Sutherland
KW9 6LR, UK
+44 (0)1408 622010
clynelishfarm.co.uk

Campsites

Brora Caravan Club
25 Saltire, Dalchalm, Brora KW9 6LP, UK
+44 (0)1408 621479
caravanclub.co.uk

Helmsdale
B&Bs

Kindale House	**Ruard Guest House**
Lilleshall Street	Stafford Street
Helmsdale, Highland	Helmsdale, Highland
KW8 6JF, UK	KW8 6JR, UK
+44 (0)1431 821415	+44 (0)1431 821013
kindalehouse.co.uk	www.ruard.co.uk

Lybster
B&Bs

Acarsaid B&B	**Bayview Hotel**
Acarsaid, Lybster Mains	Russell Street
Lybster, Caithness KW3 6AS	Lybster, Caithness KW3 6BB
+44 (0)1593 721275	+44 (0)1593 721346
acarsaidlybster.co.uk	thebayviewhotel.co.uk

Campsites

Inver Caravan Park
Houstry Road, Dunbeath, Caithness KW6 6EH, UK
+44 (0)1593 731441
inver-caravan-park.co.uk

John O'Groats
B&Bs

Hamnavoe B&B	**Seaview Hotel**
Roadside, John O'Groats,	County Road, John O'Groats,
Caithness KW1 4YR, UK	Caithness KW1 4YR, UK
+44 (0)1955 611776	+44 (0)1955 611220
johnogroatsbnb.com	seaviewjohnogroats.co.uk

Campsites

Stroma View
Huna, Wick, Caithness KW1 4YL, UK
+44 (0)1955 611313
stromaview.co.uk

Chapter Five

Cycle Shops

LEJOG 1 – Land's End to Whitecross

The Cycle Centre
1 New Street, Penzance TR18 2LZ, UK
+44 (0)1736 351671
cornwallcyclecentre.co.uk

Hayle Cycles
36 Penpol Terrace, Hayle TR27 4BQ, UK
+44 (0)1736 753825
haylecycles.com

Halfords
Unit 1, Camborne Retail Park, Camborne, Cornwall TR15 3PS, UK
+44 (0)1209 720010
halfords.com

LEJOG 2 – Whitecross to Hatherleigh

LEJOG 3 –Hatherleigh to Taunton

Kings Cycles
30 Station Rd, Taunton, Somerset TA1 1NL, UK
+44 (0)1823 352272
www.kingscycles.co.uk

The Bike Shop
30 Leat Street, Tiverton, Devon, EX16 5LG, UK
+44 (0)1884 253979

LEJOG 4 – Taunton to Clevedon

St John Street Cycles
91-93 Saint John Street, Bridgwater TA6 5HX, UK
+44 (0)1278 441500
sjscycles.co.uk

AD Cycle Repairs
58 Wakedean Gardens, Yatton, Bristol BS49 4BN, UK
+44 (0)7831 328063
adcyclerepairs.co.uk

THIS IS A MOBILE SERVICE & COULD RESCUE

LEJOG 5 – Clevedon to Gloucester

Striking Bikes
Unit 1A, Moreland Trading Estate, Bristol Road, Gloucester GL1 5RZ
+44 (0)1452 522100
striking-bikes.co.uk

LEJOG 6 – Gloucester to Kidderminster

Halfords
Oldbury Road, Tewkesbury, Gloucestershire GL20 5LZ, UK
+44 (0)1684 854990
halfords.com

Worcester Cycle Centre
8-9 College Street, Worcester WR1 2LU, UK
+44 (0)1905 611123
worcestercyclecentre.com

Dave's Cycle Repairs
24 Station Rd, Fernhill Heath, Worcester WR3 7UJ, UK
+44 (0)1905 454728
Mob: 07742081536

THIS IS A MOBILE SERVICE & COULD RESCUE

Halfords
Unit H, Crossley Retail Park, Carpet Trades Way, Kidderminster,
Worcestershire DY11 6DY, UK
+44 (0)1562 861993
halfords.com

LEJOG 7 – Kidderminster to Stoke on Trent

Hayes Cycles
42 Enville Road, Kingswinford DY6 0NL, UK
+44 (0)1384 279695

Jackson Hately Cycles Ltd
458 Stafford Road, Wolverhampton, West Midlands WV10 6AW
+44 (0)1902 782344

Specialized Concept Store
Eastgate Street, Stafford ST16 2LZ, UK
+44 (0)1785 220060

The Bike Shack
2D Radford Street, Stone ST15 8DA, UK
+44 (0)1785 816924

Vekta Velosport
Railway Enterprise Centre
Shelton New Road, Stoke-on-Trent ST4 7SH, UK
+44 (0)1782 201504
vektavelosport.co.uk

LEJOG 8 – Stoke on Trent to Hindley

Davis R & Son
22 High Street, Biddulph, Stoke-on-Trent, Staffordshire ST8 6AP
+44 (0)1782 512230

Cyclestore
36-40 West Road, Congleton, Cheshire CW12 4ES, UK
+44 (0)1260 297837
cyclestore.co.uk

Bikehaus
5 Stonepail Road, Gatley, Cheadle SK8 4EZ, UK
+44 (0)161 491 3191
wearebikehaus.co.uk

A1 Cycle Centre
414-416 Palatine Road, Wythenshawe, Manchester M22 4JT, UK
+44 (0)161 998 2882

The Bike Barn
Rifle Road, Sale M33 2LX, UK
+44 (0)7885 458473
the-bike-barn.co.uk

Halfords
Unit 1 Dacca Street, Chorley, Lancashire PR7 1EX, UK
+44 (0)1257 260408
halfords.com

Broadgate Cycle Stores
2 Hawkesbury Dr, Penwortham, Lancashire PR1 9EJ, UK
+44 (0)1772 746448
broadgatecycles.co.uk

Bowland Cycles Garstang
29 Worcester Avenue, Garstang, Preston PR3 1FJ, UK
+44 (0)1995 600194
bowlandcycles.co.uk

The Edge Cycleworks
2 Chapel Street, Lancaster, Lancashire LA1 1NZ, UK
+44 (0)1524 840800
theedgecycleworks.com

LEJOG 10 – Lancaster to Penrith

Dyno Start
1-3 Scotland Road, Carnforth, Lancashire LA5 9JY, UK
+44 (0)1524 732089
dynostart.com

Askew
The Old Brewery, Wildman Street, Kendal, Cumbria LA9 6EN
+44 (0)1539 728057
askewcycles.co.uk

Arragons Cycle Centre
2 Brunswick Road, Penrith, Cumbria CA11 7LU, UK
+44 (0)1768 890344
arragons.com

LEJOG 11 – Penrith to Lockerbie

Scotby Cycles
Church Street, Carlisle, Cumbria CA2 5TL, UK
+44 (0)1228 546931
scotbycycles.co.uk

Wheels Fargo

20 Hobart Terrace, Eastriggs, Dumfries and Galloway DG12 6QB

+44 (0)1461 700069

LEJOG 12 – Lockerbie to Carnwath

Annandale Cycles

Church Gate, Moffat, Dumfriesshire DG10 9EG, UK

+44 (0)1683 220033

annandalecycles.com

LEJOG 13 – Carnwath to Kinross

Pedal Power

13 Main St, West Calder EH55 8BY, UK

+44 (0)1506 873123

pedalpower.org.uk

Herbies Bikes Ltd

35 Drumshoreland Road, Pumpherston, Livingston EH53 0LF

+44 (0)1506 201323

herbiesbikes.co.uk

Sandy Wallace Cycles

15 Hope Street, Inverkeithing, Fife KY11 1LW, UK

+44 (0)1383 412915

swc.co.uk

Loch Leven Cycles

149 High St, Kinross, Perth and Kinross KY13 8DA, UK

+44 (0)1577 862839

lochlevencycles.co.uk

LEJOG 14 – Kinross to Blair Atholl

J. M. Richards Cycles

44 George Street, Perth PH1 5JL, UK

+44 (0)1738 626860

thecyclepeople.com

Escape Route

3 Atholl Road, Pitlochry, Perthshire PH16 5BX, UK

+44 (0)1796 473859

escape-route.co.uk

LEJOG 15 – Blair Atholl to Aviemore

Mikes Bikes
5A Myrtlefield, Aviemore, Highland PH22 1SB, UK
+44 (0)1479 810478
aviemorebikes.co.uk

LEJOG 16 – Aviemore to Evanton

Alpine Bikes Inverness
2 Henderson Road, Inverness IV1 1SN, UK
+44 (0)1463 729171
alpinebikes.com

Dryburgh Cycles
6 Tulloch Street, Dingwall IV15 9JY, UK
+44 (0)1349 862163
dryburghcycles.co.uk

LEJOG 17 – Evanton to Helmsdale

The Mellow Velo
75 High Street, Alness, Ross-shire IV17 0SH, UK
+44 (0)1349 883141
themellowvelo.com

LEJOG 18 – Helmsdale to John O'Groats

The Spot Cycle Shop
Wick, Caithness, UK
+44 (0)1955 602698
thespotcycles.co.uk

Appendix One

Links to Google Maps

Listed below are links to the routes on Google Maps.

If you need a google account to access the maps you should be prompted to set one up.

Once you have opened a map you can zoom in and out to get finer detail than the screen shots in this book.

You can bookmark the map to your own My Places by clicking on Save to My Places.

LEJOG 1 – Land's End to Whitecross
https://tinyurl.com/lands-white
LEJOG 2 – Whitecross to Hatherleigh
https://tinyurl.com/white-hatherleigh
LEJOG 3 – Hatherleigh to Taunton
https://tinyurl.com/hatherleigh-taunton
LEJOG 4 – Taunton to Clevedon
https://tinyurl.com/taunton-clevedon
LEJOG 5 – Clevedon to Gloucester
https://tinyurl.com/clevedon-gloucester
LEJOG 6 – Gloucester to Kidderminster
https://tinyurl.com/gloucester-kidderminster
LEJOG 7 – Kidderminster to Stoke-on-Trent
https://tinyurl.com/Kidderminster-stoke
LEJOG 8 – Stoke-on-Trent to Hindley
https://tinyurl.com/stoke-hindley

LEJOG 9 – Hindley to Lancaster
https://tinyurl.com/hindley-lancaster
LEJOG 10 – Lancaster to Penrith
https://tinyurl.com/lancaster-penrith
LEJOG 11 – Penrith to Lockerbie
https://tinyurl.com/penrith-lockerbie
LEJOG 12 – Lockerbie to Carnwath
https://tinyurl.com/lockerbie-carnwath
LEJOG 13 – Carnwath to Kinross
https://tinyurl.com/carnwath-kinross
LEJOG 14 – Kinross to Blair Atholl
https://tinyurl.com/kinross-blair
LEJOG 15 – Blair Atholl to Aviemore
https://tinyurl.com/blair-aviemore
LEJOG 16 – Aviemore to Evanton
https://tinyurl.com/aviemore-evanton
LEJOG 17 – Evanton to Helmsdale
https://tinyurl.com/evanton-helmsdale
LEJOG 18 – Helmsdale to John O'Groats
https://tinyurl.com/helmsdale-john

Appendix Two
Re-Routing Using a Garmin 800

The technique described below may work in a similar way on other Garmin models and on other sat navs and navigation devices but they have not been tested.

What do you do if you are navigating a route or course using your Garmin 800 and you get lost? Perhaps you lost concentration and suddenly realise that you should have made a turn and are now miles away from the route. Do you retrace your steps? Or should you use the 'recalculate route' function?

The answer is probably neither.

There is probably a quicker way back to your intended route than following back the way you have just come. If nothing else, retracing your steps is demoralising. But you shouldn't use the recalculate route option either.

When I first started using a sat nav I thought that if I got lost and rerouted then the sat nav would take me back to the closest part of my loaded route, after all, if I was using a paper map that is what I would do. Unfortunately the sat nav is not that sophisticated: it will simply take the point where you are and your final destination and then plot a new route between the two, based upon the settings you have given it (things like avoid highways, avoid tolls etc..). This is unlikely to be the same route you loaded, especially if you are on a circular route.

So how can you navigate back to the route without losing the original navigation on your route?

Step One

Flick through the screens on your Garmin until you locate the map screen. Zoom the view out by clicking on the '-' symbol until you can see your route. By eye locate a point on your route where you

could re-join it. Then zoom in on the point using the '+'. You will probably have to move around on the map if you are some distance from your route. To do this click on the 'arrows' symbol and then drag your finger around the screen to move the map.

Step Two

Once you have located the point where you would like to re-join the route and zoomed in to get sufficient detail, press that point on the screen with your finger. A large pin should appear. You can drag it around if it is not quite in

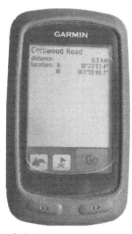

the right place.

Step Three

Now press the location name box or the symbol with three lines at the top of the screen. A new screen will appear giving a grid reference for the point and the distance to it (in a straight line). Click on the Go button at the bottom of the screen.

Step Four

The sat nav will now navigate you to the selected point. Once you reach that point and re-join your original route the sat nav should then automatically continue navigating along that route.

You can also use this technique to navigate around impassable obstructions, such as closed roads (although few are closed enough to stop a determined cyclist) or obstructed paths. You may have to do a two part operation though, one to take you away from the obstruction and another to get you back to the route, otherwise the sat nav will probably just route you through the obstruction again, after all, it doesn't know it is there!

Figure 15 - Ruthven Barracks, Highlands

Other Books

LEJOG Self Help Cycle Guide

If this book has inspired you to take up the challenge of riding from Land's End to John O'Groats yourself then you may be interested in Royston's: Land's End to John O'Groats Self Help Cycle Guide.

The guide has helped thousands of readers with tips and advice about:
- How to get to the start/from the finish
- Where you are going to sleep
- Equipment - what you need to take with you
- Nutrition - what you should eat and drink
- How much training you need to do
- Route creation including how to create your own personalised route with gpx file using Google Maps

The book is available as:

    Paperback at Amazon
    Kindle at Amazon
    E book at iBooks
    E book at Smashwords
    PDF at www.landsend-to-johnogroats.co.uk

Also available worldwide from various online retailers.

LEJOG Cycling the Google Route

This is a travelogue style account of Royston's first ride across the country when creating the route contained in this book.

Whilst it is not exactly the route in this book, because it has been re-routed since, it gives a good impression of the type of experience you will have. The route described is about 90% the same, the other 10% being the dodgy bits that the route in this book has bypassed!

The book is available as:

> Paperback at Amazon
> Kindle at Amazon
> PDF at www.landsend-to-johnogroats.co.uk

Also available worldwide from various online retailers.

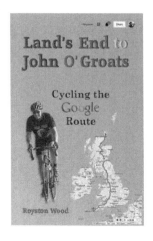